Forest of Ash:
The Earliest Written Basque Poetry

Bidart Family Collection No.3

# Forest of Ash:
## The Earliest Written Basque Poetry

Translations by
Xabier Irujo and David Romtvedt

Introduction by
Xabier Irujo

Preface by
Daavid Romtvedt

Center for Basque Studies
University of Nevada, Reno
2024

*This book was published with the generous support of the Bidart family and the Government of Bizkaia.*

Library of Congress Cataloging-in-Publication Data

Names:
Irujo Ametzaga, Xabier, translator, writer of introduction.
Romtvedt, David, translator, writer of preface.
Title: Forest of ash : the earliest written Basque poetry /
translations by Xabier Irujo and David Romtvedt; introduction by
Xabier Irujo; preface by David Romtvedt.
Description: Reno : Center for Basque Studies Press, 2024.

Series: Bidart Family Collection series; 3
Includes bibliographical references and index.

Summary: "Forest of Ash offers to English language readers many of the oldest known fragments of poems and songs in Basque, bits and pieces of a distant time, place, and language. While the work is more literary than scholarly - more a collection of poems that can live, breathe, and speak to us now than an examination of the world in which the poems first lived - multilingual readers may wish to consult works of Basque scholarship that can broaden our understanding of the poems and their first world. Such works include: Euskal baladak: azterketa eta edizio kritikoa by Jabier Kaltzakorta, La puerta abierta: baladas vascas e internacionales by Alan Griffin, and Anthology of Basque Oral Literature by Xabier Paya"-- Provided by publisher.

Identifiers: LCCN 2024007218 | ISBN 9781949805857 (paperback)
Subjects: LCSH: Basque poetry--Translations into English.
LCGFT: Poetry.
Classification: LCC PH5397.E3 F67 2024 | DDC 899/.92108--dc23/eng/20240404
LC record available at https://lccn.loc.gov/2024007218

# Contents

Introduction .................................................................9

Preface........................................................................18

Beotibarko kantua /
The Song of Beotibar .................................................32

Urruxolako guduaren kanta /
Song of the Battle of Urruxola..................................37

Akondiako kanta / Song of Akondia.........................41

Ahetzeko anderearen kanta /
The Lady of Ahetze's Song........................................ 44

Ahetzeko anderearen kanta (bigarren bertsioa) /
The Lady of Ahetze's Song (second version)..............53

Bereterretxeren kanta /
Bereterretxe's Song .....................................................58

Peru Abendañoren edo Aramaioko guduaren kanta /
Peru Abendaño's Song or The Battle of Aramaio......66

Arrasateko erreketako kanta /
Song of the Burning of Arrasate ................................70

Errodrigo Zaratekoaren kanta /
Rodrigo of Zarate's Song............................................77

Sanda Ilia / Saint Elijah ............................................81

Juana, Muxikako eta Butroeko alabaren kanta /
The Song of Juana, daughter of Muxika
and Butron ................................................................86

Ozaetako Santxaren edo Martin Bañezen kanta /
Santxa of Ozaeta's or Martin Bañez's Song...............90

Martin Ibañez Labierokoaren hilartitza /
Martin Ibañez Labiero's Tombstone .........................94

Salinasko kontea preso sartu zuteneko kanta /
The Song of Those Who Captured
the Count of Salinas ...................................................... 98

Domenjon de Andiaren kantua /
Domenjon Andia's Song ................................................ 102

Juan Lazkanoren kanta /
Juan Lazkano's Song .................................................... 106

Bretainiako kanta / The Song of Brittany ................ 110

Milia Lasturkoren eresia /
The Elegy for Milia of Lastur ..................................... 116

Jançu janto dego de garcigorreta /
You Eat, We'll Eat, the Freeloaders' Ball ................ 122

Çutegon / On My Feet ................................................. 128

Un señora muerto habías
(Juantxo Mondragonen kantua)/
My Lady, You've Killed
(Juantxo Mondragon's Song) ..................................... 132

Nafarroako kondestablearen kanta /
The Governor General of Navarre's Song .............. 136

Leloren kanta / Lelo's Song ........................................ 141

Une mousse de Biscaye / A Basque Girl ................. 148

Perutxoren kanta / Perutxo's Song ........................... 155

Alostorrea / The Alos Tower ..................................... 158

Testamentuaren balada / Last Words ....................... 168

Atarratzeko jauregian / In the Atarratze Palace ..... 172

Atarratzeko jauregian (bigarren bertsioa) /
In the Atarratze Palace (second version) ................. 178

Bibliography ................................................................. 185

Notes .............................................................................. 189

# Introduction
# Literature, A Mirror to History

While imprisoned in the tower of Muñatones (Muskiz, Bizkaia) in the early 1470s, Lope de García Salazar—the "first historian of Bizkaia"—wrote his twenty-five-volume *Istoria de las bienandanças e fortunas* covering world history from the biblical creation to the mid-fifteenth century. Although he mixed myth and fact, the last section of his work is considered one of the main sources documenting the nearly one hundred years of war that devastated the Basque Country from 1362 to 1457.

Explaining the roots of various conflicts, García Salazar notes that during May Day religious processions, local brotherhoods carried huge candles to churches. During one of these processions, participants from Murua (in Zigoitia, Araba) wanted to carry the candles low—at foot height (*oina*)—while those from Ulibarri (in Arratzua-Ubarrundia, Araba) wanted to carry them high—at neck height (*ganboa*). The disagreement between the two groups—the Oiñaz and the Ganboa—escalated to the point of violence with deaths on both sides.

The real root of these wars rests in the various crises caused by the Plague of 1348—the Black Death. Extreme demographic changes led to widespread social instability resulting in conflicts such as the Hundred Years' War, the Jacquerie, the Ciompi Revolt, and the Bohemian Hussite insurrections. Similar effects were seen in the Basque Country where in a few months the Plague killed nearly half the population of the Kingdom of Navarre—140,000 people. Vast numbers also died in the other Basque territories of Araba, Bizkaia, Lapurdi, Gipuzkoa, and Zuberoa. The ensuing crisis in agricultural production led to poverty and famine. Large areas—both rural and urban—were practically uninhabited. Repopulation was accompanied by conflict that was exacerbated by special interests and power struggles.

The great families—the *ahaide nagusiak* or noble, wealthy houses—often loosely linked by blood ties, were increasingly at odds with one another. In Gipuzkoa, such inter-family conflicts were crystallized in the factions of Oiñaz and Ganboa. The factions came to be represented by the Beaumonts and Agramonts in Navarre. The constant aggression of Castile against Navarre fueled these rivalries. Notwithstanding various defections and changing of sides, Oiñaz and Beaumont generally supported Castile, while Ganboa and Agramont were more aligned with the Crown of Navarre. In addition to conflicts driven by Castilian actions, there was rising tension between members of the nobility, between the nobility and the peasantry, and between the rural nobility and the rising cities.

In the words of Lope de García Salazar, who sided with Oiñaz, these fights were driven by greed, "to know who was worth more on the land." Or, as Juan Victoria said in the sixteenth century, to know "who was worth more and was deemed to command the rest." In Basque, this was expressed by the Fruniz family motto, as recorded in *The Ibarguen-Cachopín Chronicle* (1558-1610)—"Guerrea espa baquea, gustia da enea" (Arriolabengoa, 1996). In war and in peace, everything is mine.

Many Basques, whether in the country, small towns, or cities, viewed the noble families as enemies of the people—criminals whose activities damaged society, the economy, and the well-being of the people. In response, these critics of the nobility formed defensive bands that often engaged in banditry, thus further destabilizing society. The Crown and city governments organized leagues to confront what they saw as lawless gangs. This gave rise to the brotherhoods ruled by the *foruak*, the traditional laws of the Basque Country.

Longstanding hostilities ended abruptly in July 1456 when Juan Lopez Lazkano, Martin Ruiz Ganboa, Ladron Balda, and a long list of rebel noblemen nailed "the challenge of Azkoitia" to the southeast door of the Idiakez Tower—the city's gate. Their challenge called on residents of not only Azkoitia but the other Gipuzkoan towns of Azpeitia, Deba, Mutriku, Getaria, Tolosa, Ordizia, and Segura to arm themselves and solve their differences in duels. The brotherhoods rebelled against both sides and turned to King Enrique IV for help. The king banished both the Ganboa and the Oiñaz groups and ordered that all noblemen be sent to the Andalusian border for one to four years to fight against the Iberian Peninsula's Muslim rulers. The king also ordered the demolition or topping of the noblemen's towers.

While Enrique's orders strengthened the cities and the brotherhoods, violent conflict continued until 1479 when a group of troops and horsemen attacked the Lazkano Tower in Kontrasta (Araba) and killed Juan Lopez Lazkano, one of the leaders of the Oiñaz family. In Navarre, the last chapter of the war between bands occurred when the Beaumonts, betraying their legitimate queen, Katalina (Catherine), supported the troops of Castile and Aragon in their conquest of the kingdom of Navarre between 1512 and 1522.

Most of the poems in this book that were written in the fifteenth century deal with particular chapters of these wars. These include the first sixteen poems and "The Governor General of Navarre's Song," all of which are set during the wars and introduce the *ahaide nagusiak* as characters. Most of them are quite partisan songs of hatred, revenge, jealousy, and self-interest. Fear and terror come from the mouths of characters on both sides.

Such is the case of the moving "Song of the Burning of Arrasate." Pero Belez Gebara, unable to take the city of Arrasate by siege, orders it set on fire—with the intention of killing those who, fleeing the flames, would try to escape the city. While the song recounts how the city was razed, it begins with harsh verses against some members of the Oiñaz band who did not come to help in battle. Later, the author mentions the dead heroes and reproaches the Ganboans whom he identifies as perfidious and cowardly. The poem ends with a mention of the cowardice of the Lord of Ozaeta, a supporter of the Oiñaz band, who escaped from the battlefield leaving his people behind.

Some of the poets sing about the nonsensical death and destruction that occurred. Some speak on behalf of the brotherhoods and their efforts to pacify the land, as in "Domenjon Andia's Song" honoring Domenjon Andia, head of the Brotherhood of Gipuzkoa in 1456. The verses allude to Domenjon's kindness toward the good, humble people of the land with whom he is as "sweet as an apple," and to his energy when confronting the wicked noblemen, in front of whom he wields his sword.

Aside from the songs recalling the massacres of war, and perhaps as a reaction to such cruelty, the experience and views of women emerge vividly in these earliest surviving examples of Basque poetry. Female figures are at the center of six of the poems: "The Lady of Ahetze's Song," "Bereterretxe's Song," "The Song of Juana, daughter of Muxika and Butron," "Santxa of Ozaeta's or Martin Bañez's Song," "The Elegy for Milia of Lastur," and "In the Atarratze Palace." These poems are sung by women who face a dilemma of life and death. Some of them—Juana Muxika and Santxa Ozaeta, for example—exert their legal right and responsibility to act independently as heads of families (analogous to that of men in terms of owning and transferring property).

Santxa Otxoa Ozaeta, Lady of Mendijur and Maturana, bitterly laments the death of her husband, Martin Bañez Artazubiaga, one of the seven Ganboan warriors sentenced to death for the burning of Arrasate in 1448. But what stands out are the last three verses in which she demands revenge. The people of Ganboa never forgave the murderers or their allies and, far from succumbing to grief over the loss of her husband, she expresses her intention—as head of family—to burn the village of Aramaio, home of her enemies, to the ground.

This contrasts with the view of Juana, Lady of Muxika and Butron, who, in love with Martin Ruiz, Lord of Olaso and a Ganboa leader who also participated in the siege and burning of Arrasate, confronts her family and marries her beloved Martin. She reproaches her mother who would stop the marriage, saying that following the death of her father, she is the rightful heir. The main theme of this fragment is the importance of complying with the word of the father and with the rule of law. Under medieval Basque law, women had the right to inherit, hold, and administer their properties before, during, and after marriage, and in widowhood. In fact, according to the Code of Laws of Estella (c. 1076), one of the first written legal documents in the history of the Basque Country, women were legal subjects and could be "heads of the family" with the same rights and duties as men.

The figure of Marisantz Buztanobi stands out in the exquisite "Bereterretxe's Song." Marisantz is the mother who does everything possible to save her son who has been arrested by the bloodthirsty Count of Lerin, the rebel leader of the Beaumont faction who had betrayed the Queen of Navarre. Marisantz runs through the mountains to the house of her brother Buztanobi in Lakarri. She then crosses the five peaks of the Bosmendieta mountain range and descends to the Andotze Valley, traveling twenty miles on foot to the city of Maule in one night. It is there that the count cruelly tells her about the death of her son: "Go, bring him back to life." Unlike the count, Marisantz, exercising her rights and complying with the law, recovers her son Bereterretxe's body. The Count of Lerin's crime is symbolized by Bereterretxe's blood-stained shirt which Margarita Ezpeldoi, his lover, tries to clean.

"The Elegy for Milia of Lastur" describes the death in Arrasate of the young Milia during childbirth. Such medieval dirges were sung by women, which explains why it is Milia's unnamed sister who opens the story, contending that Peru Gartzia has not treated his wife well, and expressing her wish that he return Milia's lifeless body to be buried in her hometown. She does not hide her resentment towards the people of Arrasate-Mondragón for the pain they've brought the women of Gipuzkoa. The first lines of the poem are deeply moving: "What follows the pain of giving birth? / Baked apple and rosé wine. / Not so for Milia, cold earth / below, gravestone above."

The poems "The Lady of Ahetze's Song" and "In the Atarratze Palace" also deal with themes closely related to women's rights. In the first, Domenja denounces the jealousy of her husband, Menauton Urrutia, and the mistreatment to which she is being subjected. The poem is, from this perspective, a critique of gender violence or domestic abuse. Menauton accuses his wife of adultery and drags her by the hair across the floor of their house. She claims to be innocent, but he is not willing to believe her, and she lives in sadness, with "her head on the pillow, / her heart far away." In the second version of the poem, the abusive husband is driven from the house by Domenja's brother who thus guarantees both justice and his sister's right to not be mistreated.

"In the Atarratze Palace" deals with women's rights regarding marriage. The poem describes the 1587 marriage of Charles de Luxe and Maria Jaurgain in the town of Atarratze (Zuberoa). Maria was seventeen while her husband Charles was already a mature man who between 1567 and 1570 had led the rebellion of the Catholic lords against the Queen of Navarre, Joana d'Albret, in her attempt to promote the Protestant reform. Defeated, the de Luxe family went into exile and only after the queen's death in 1572 could they return to Zuberoa. According to Orpustan, and other authors, the poem intertwines various stories and legends, giving rise to different versions, but what transcends all the stories and unites various versions of the poem is the main theme: the Lord of Ozaze organizes the marriage of one of his two daughters to a rich elderly man against her will. She loves another man and on the wedding day commits suicide by jumping from a window. The poem echoes the old Basque law that forbade grandparents and parents from arranging the marriages of their grandchildren and children without their consent.

The last poems, those that can be dated to the beginning of the sixteenth century, are love poems in which, unlike the previous works, authors add a humorous ingredient. This includes "My Lady, You've Killed (Juantxo Mondragon's Song)," and "A Basque Girl." These two poems, together with "You Eat, We'll Eat, the Freeloaders' Ball," were originally collected in the *Cancionero de Palacio* (a compilation of court music and poetry) and later published by Francisco Asenjo Barbieri in 1890. Since they are transcriptions made by authors who had no knowledge of the Basque language or, as in the case of "My Lady, You've Killed," who had little knowledge of Spanish, these poems offer certain grammatical problems. "You Eat, We'll Eat, the Freeloaders' Ball" is the most extreme case, a poem transcribed "by hearsay" by a person who did not speak Basque and, therefore, its meaning remains a mystery to this day.

"A Basque Girl" was first published in 1503 by Ottaviano Petrucci in the Venice edition of his work *Harmonices Musices Odhecaton*. Rabelais quoted the poem in his work *La vie de Gargantua et de Pantagruel*, published between 1532 and 1564. It is a poem written in French that introduces a verse in the Basque language, in the mouth of a beautiful Basque shepherdess who rejects the love proposal of a French gentleman who does not speak her language. Some scholars who have interpreted this poem believe it to be a scene of sexual harassment rather than a comedic encounter.

It has been said that literature is the most suggestive way to ignore life, but it's certainly not true of these poems. The Basque poets of the fifteenth and sixteenth centuries sang about the events of their lives using the forms of expression and the social and cultural viewpoints of their time. Reading these poems, we discover that the desires and pains of those who suffered so intensely or who loved with so much passion in that corner of the world we call the Basque Country, are indeed universal. Herein lies the magic of literature. Through it, we realize that no one is alone or isolated in the universe. Most of the events narrated by these anonymous poets six centuries ago could be episodes in our current lives, experienced with the same passion and emotion. The poems in the present book offer a mirror of the experiences and miseries of these people, a mirror reflecting a chapter in the history of humankind, a specific moment in a specific place on earth. They serve as humanity's memory. Their music will express forever what cannot be silenced because it is in the hearts of all of us.

Xabier Irujo
Reno, Nevada, fall 2023

# Preface
# Forest of Ash

*Forest of Ash* offers to English language readers many of the oldest known fragments of poems and songs in Basque, bits and pieces of a distant time, place, and language. While the work is more literary than scholarly—more a collection of poems that can live, breathe, and speak to us now than an examination of the world in which the poems first lived—multilingual readers may wish to consult works of Basque scholarship that can broaden our understanding of the poems and their first world. Such works include: *Euskal baladak: azterketa eta edizio kritikoa* by Xabier Kaltzakorta, *La puerta abierta: baladas vascas e internacionales* by Alan Griffin, and *Anthology of Basque Oral Literature* by Xabier Paya.

While recognizing the scholarly interest we may have in these poems, in translating them with Xabier Irujo, I have sought to honor their power to resist the passage of time, however ravaged they may be by that passage. For some of the poems, we have only a single line—a tiny window through which the light shines, illuminating an isolated scene, a discreet moment, a sudden suggestion. This is the case for the poem "Akondiako kanta" (translated here as "Song of Akondia") of which three words are all that remain. *Acundia lejarr[a]ga lejarbaga*—Akondia, forest of ash, the absent trees.

Let us look more deeply at the word *ash*, a metaphoric marker for this collection of poems. *Lejar* in the medieval Basque of the poem and *lizar* in Batua—contemporary Unified Basque—is one of many species of trees that covers the mountains and lines the watercourses of the Basque Country. For Basques whose livelihood has long been based on fishing and farming, whose spirituality has been strongly linked to nature, and whose leisure time has often been spent mountaineering, forests are central to identity and survival. Given their relatively long lives, trees are a bridge joining the past to the present.

The most famous Basque tree is not an ash but an oak—the Gernika oak under which for centuries invaders, would be rulers, and both committed and ambivalent allies came to swear loyalty to the *foruak*, the laws that ruled the Basque Country.

While it's not as famous as the Gernika oak, ash is integral to the biological web of life in the Basque Country. And it's increasingly under attack. Because of the relatively low level of tannins in its leaves, it's less resistant to the emerald ash borer—an insect that has decimated many forests. Ash is also vulnerable to attack from an invasive fungus that has caused a serious dieback of forests throughout Europe. Other pressures are exerted on ash by the growing human population and the consequent diminution of the tree's habitat. If ash were to disappear, hundreds of other life forms would disappear with it—lichens, mosses, fungi, and various species of birds. Ash seen this way reflects the sensibility that drives poetry both in the medieval Basque Country and in the translations that make up this book.

In "Akondiako kanta," the ash have been destroyed and so the forest has no trees. We often blame loss on outside forces, and indeed outside forces press on both the non-human inhabitants of the Basque Country— the air and water, the plants and animals—and on the Basque people, threatening their language and culture while limiting their political and social autonomy.

But the medieval destruction at Akondia was caused not so much by outside forces as by Basques fighting each other, the result of ongoing long-term conflict between various families and communities. In this case, the Ganboa and Ibarguen families laid siege to the Unzueta Tower in Eibar, Gipuzkoa, the combatants facing one another on the slopes of Mount Akondia. No outside army had invaded. The Roman empire had fallen long ago, and the Islamic caliphate was nearing its end. The rising nation states of France and Spain sent no troops. At Akondia, Basque fought Basque, proving, as has been proven so many times and in so many places, that we need no external enemy to help us destroy ourselves.

Centuries after the battle at Akondia, we see this fear of self destruction expressed in the song "Aita semeak," the first stanza of which appeared in Juan Antonio Mogel Urkiza's book *Peru Abarka*—dialogues between an urban professor and a rural bachelor. Written in 1802 but not published until 1880, Urquiza's longing for what he saw as a traditional way of life was reinforced in the 1970s by new lyrics focused on who's to blame if Basque culture and the Basque language cease to exist. In one of these new lyrics, thieves have taken everything in the house, leaving us half naked and, as always, under the thumb of someone else. But another lyric contends that the fault is our own, that we have no one to blame but ourselves if the Basque Country disappears. Whether in the fourteenth century poetry collection *Forest of Ash*, the nineteenth century novel *Peru Abarka*, or the late twentieth century song "Aita semeak," we find concerns about the extinction of all things Basque and about who is to blame.

Another concern that is quite present in *Forest of Ash* arises from the power and futility of revenge as a motivating force in human interaction. We see this in "Peru Abendaño's Song," also known as "The Battle of Aramaio." Here, the king of Castile's first crossbowman leads troops to the Bizkaian town of Otxandio to burn the fortress of the Butron family. From Otxandio, the attackers go to Aramaio where they burn twenty houses, leading to a revenge battle in which one man is impaled on a spear and dragged along the ground by the hair until dead. The killer's intention to burn the body is stopped only by the intervention of a group of women who urge the attackers to not waste time with the dead, but instead help the living.

It is not only Aramaio and Otxandio that are burned. In Arrasate, attackers lay siege to the town, demanding its surrender. The townspeople refuse, and when the siege fails, the attackers form a perimeter line and set the entire community on fire. When the defenders, along with the trapped locals, flee the flames, they're all killed.

Aramaio, Otxandio, and Arrasate were three among many towns destroyed by fire. In the ten years between 1437 and 1447, Mungia, Zumarraga, Azkoitia, Elgeta, Berastegi, Legazpia, and Larrabetzu were also burned. Otxandio was burned twice. All reduced to ash.

It's fire that marks the poem "Saint Elijah," too. Here, a muleteer is robbed of his cargo of wine and of his cash. He reports the theft to the local authorities who send deputies to investigate. The thieves, operating under the protection of a local criminal gang leader, retreat to the nearby cave of the prophet Saint Elijah where, after another failed siege, the deputies start a fire hoping to smoke the fugitives out.

While many of the medieval poems and songs that have survived to the present chronicle destruction and loss, it would be misleading to suggest that this tells the whole story. "The Lady of Ahetze's Song" addresses a woman's suffering at the hands of her jealous, suspicious, and abusive husband who through an unlikely miracle is finally awakened to the honesty and goodness of his wife.

"In the Atarratze Palace" presents a young woman who refuses an arranged marriage to a very rich and very old man. We include two examples of the story. In one, the rich old man is the Lord of Atarratze. It's a fine match as long as one isn't concerned with human feeling. But the young bride-to-be is and accuses her mother of selling her like a calf to be shipped off to Spain. In the other rendering of the story, the rich old man is the King of Hungary and it's the father who would sell his daughter, this time, she tells us, like an ox. In both poems the young woman wants to make her own choice—to marry for love.

"The Alos Tower" includes elements of the Cinderella story—a young woman living in poverty and unremitting labor whose life is suddenly changed to one of remarkable fortune following her marriage to a nobleman, usually a king, and her own ascension to nobility. The Basque version of this, told more than a hundred years before what is often considered the first European publication of the story in Italy in 1634, focuses on the mistreatment of the Cinderella character and the more active intervention of the father in defense of his daughter.

We begin with the usual happy family—father, mother, and beloved daughter. Then comes the disaster that is detailed in similar stories found around the world—the mother dies, the widowed husband and father remarries, the new wife is cruel to her stepdaughter. Here the stories diverge. While not overtly condemning his new wife, the loving Basque father attempts to protect his daughter by arranging her marriage to a local man many consider to be a fool or crazy. As unlikely as it seems, the marriage works out with the daughter saying she would have no better man. The protection is only temporary, though, as the father is called away to war and in his absence the stepmother writes to him to report that his beloved daughter has given birth to an illegitimate son and therefore shamed the family name. Of course we know who actually had an extramarital affair and gave birth to the boy. The husband away at war has his suspicions and returns home where he fakes his death in a fanciful scheme to find the truth. In the end, the daughter's integrity and fortune is confirmed with the unmasking of the stepmother and her lover, the latter killed by the father rising from the dead.

Various experiences of love are recounted again and again—the exemplary brothers and sisters, the virtuous husbands and wives, the devoted mothers and fathers. The not-so-loving also make an appearance—the self-centered seducer and the abuser. "A Basque Girl" gives us a young woman who defends herself from the advances of a French dandy, confusing him by speaking only Basque. Royal marriages consolidate kingdoms. There is love reduced to the sham of trivial sexual escapades. One poem includes prose passages in which an unidentified speaker mocks society's self-proclaimed elites, exposing the pretensions of an impoverished nobleman who fancies himself above ordinary mortals. This gentleman complains that he can't afford a servant and so has to take care of his horse himself. But he doesn't, so the horse goes uncared for while the gentleman spends his time chasing women.

A parent's loss appears when a young man is kidnapped by his political enemies. Claiming they are taking him to the authorities, the kidnappers tie their captive to a tree and fire two arrows into him. The young man's mother walks through the night seeking news of her dead son. Blood fills a servant's hands as she washes the dead man's shirt. Maybe the servant is the dead man's lover. It may as well be three dozen bloody shirts.

Social and political themes are also addressed in these fragments—trade relations between Gipuzkoa and England, the early development of democratic institutions in commerce and government, the formation of the first trade unions, the actions of an honorable political leader who brought peace to Gipuzkoa.

Finally, reminding us that comedy has its place, there are two or three joking pieces—depending on what one considers to be a joke. One clearly comedic piece is a sea shanty: sailors singing as they row, joking about who's lazy and weak, about who can do the job, about sex, about good food, and about poverty-stricken university students crashing parties for the free food. The second comedic piece narrates the lament of a lover who finds love is too much and who says, "I'm on my feet but can't stand still." Finally, there is a poem narrated by a Frenchman frustrated in his attempt to seduce a Basque girl. But it's unclear if that last poem is meant to be funny.

Whatever the subject or style, most of the songs and poems have come to us anonymously, their authors and composers forever unknown, their stories passed along orally from person to person for long periods before being written down. In some cases it was centuries before a song appeared in print, sometimes in several variants. Whether we have one version or several, whatever was finally transcribed and appeared on the printed page may only slightly reflect the intention, the language, the melodies, or the psyche of the original writers and composers.

This brings us to the problems and privileges of translation. Let's return to ash, both the tree and the gray powdery material left when a fire has consumed its fuel. An English speaker hearing the word ash may picture both a tree and the remnants of a fire. Or the fire itself. The two kinds of ash identified by the same word end up jammed together so that the English title *Forest of Ash* suggests both the beauty and grandeur of a forest and the loss of the forest through fire. While we can't say whether the poetry we have in *Forest of Ash* is generally reflective of Basque medieval literature, it's striking how often what we have deals with loss. And how often this loss is the result of brutal conflict. Only ash left to us.

Of course this talk about ash as a tree and as the remnants of a fire would have no meaning for a Basque speaker, neither of the fifteenth century nor the twenty-first, as the ash tree is *lizar* while the ash that remains after a fire is *hauts* or *errauts*. The tree and the fire don't share the same word. And *lizardi*, the literal translation of ash forest is only that—*lizardi*.

We see in a single word the impossibility of bringing one language seamlessly into another. Each word is a microcosm of a language's way of responding to ideas and experience, a particular way of seeing and being in the world. Linguistic diversity shows the breadth of the human mind and so helps us to be flexible in the face of environmental and social challenges while revealing the strong links between language and identity. How much of our being is the result of the language we use? Did we create our language, or did it create us?

While I've claimed that it is impossible to bring one language seamlessly into another, that's what I long to do as a translator. I would give the English-language reader versions of the poems that reflect as accurately as possible the consciousness and experience of those Basque singers and poets from five, six, and seven hundred years ago.

But what is accuracy in the translation of a poem? It can't be only the faithful rendering of the literal meaning of a text, as poems are often as much about sound as meaning. Should our translation then use as many of the same sounds as possible in both languages? The same rhythms? What about rhyme? Should a poem that rhymes in Basque rhyme in its English translation? If we can find an English tree whose name rhymes with *lizar*, should we use it? Poplar? But the accent's in the wrong place. And it doesn't feel right to change the species of tree even in pursuit of the rhyme or the avoidance of the double meaning of ash.

What about metaphors? Let's say a contemporary poet writes that someone speaks like an announcer on EITB. EITB is the Basque Autonomous Community's public broadcast service. Many English language readers would be unfamiliar with the acronym. In the United States, we could say NPR and in Great Britain the BBC. Does that mean we need to translate to a locally meaningful metaphor for each English language community—ABC in Australia, CBC in Canada, NTA in Nigeria? Maybe stick with EITB and put a note in the back of the book.

More generally, should translations of medieval Basque poetry give the feeling of medieval Basque speech and thought? Can this be done through contemporary English? And what happens when we're translating a fragment that seems to have something beautiful or important to say but in our estimation doesn't say it very well? Does the translator have the right to improve the original poem? Perhaps we imagine that if we make just a few changes, the poem will be much better. Whose poem is it, anyway? Most questions asked about what makes for a true, correct, accurate translation have few absolute answers. Perhaps no translation will ever be completely right. Still, we keep trying, and some translations feel better than others, more right, even if we can't say how accurate they are.

Again, let's take *lizar* as ash. The translation is accurate as to the name of the tree, but misleading because of the suggestion of fire that is present in English but absent in Basque. I mentioned changing ash to poplar possibly for a sound echo of *lizar* and possibly to avoid the double meaning of ash. We could also change ash to ponderosa pine—a common tree in the western United States. In the forests above my home in Buffalo, Wyoming, a town deeply shaped by Basque immigration, I often hike or bicycle through stands of these pine. I sometimes stop, lean close to one of the great trees, and press my face against the bark to take in the rich sweet smell. Some people say it's butterscotch. Others say vanilla or cinnamon. One friend tells me the tree evokes for him his childhood—the scent of his mother's kitchen when she baked cookies. A few people claim the smell is coconut. If I translated *lizar* as ponderosa pine, I would be making a very strong pitch for bringing the poem not only into English but into the Wyoming Basque world of the late twentieth and early twenty-first centuries. I would be putting my bet on the importance of evoking the translation's physical place, the feel of the poem for the contemporary English language reader in a single, small, Basque American community. As to literal accuracy—oops.

I go on speaking of the problems of translation, the associations we feel between a word, an experience, and a memory. In many ways, a translation is a new poem in a different language, a poem that has been inspired by the original.

For most of its history, Basque was a spoken language only. Thousands of years without writing—no grammar or dictionary to consult, no language academy to define and govern "correct" usage, no seeing sounds as graphic symbols or as abstract pictures of actions and objects. It seems to me that for speakers of a language with no written form, words must be more closely aligned to music than for speakers whose language is shaped by reading and writing. But I just made this up and maybe I'm wrong. We might do best to consult a paleo-linguist or an ethnomusicologist.

Another translation issue arises from the fact of English being a global language, one that is widely used as a result of political, economic, and linguistic imperialism over hundreds of years. Basque, on the other hand, is a minority language which has been discouraged by the French and Spanish governments under which the Basques have lived for centuries. Sometimes the degree of discouragement has been very great indeed—the thirty-six years, for example, in which the Franco dictatorship in Spain made it illegal to use Basque in public discourse—no books or magazines, no newspapers, no television or radio, no poems recited, and no songs sung in Basque. Or the insistence on the part of the French Republics that the language of instruction in public schools be French only. In such circumstances a language goes underground. Pressured to speak French or Spanish, Basque was used almost solely among trusted family members and friends. It marked insider and outsider, wielder of power and subject of power. To speak it was to engage in a form of political and social resistance to foreign rule.

I experienced this long before I had any idea that my life would include marriage into a Basque American family. I was bicycling in what I thought of as France—the Northern Basque Country—and crossed the Pyrenees into what I thought of as Spain—the Southern Basque Country. It was the early 1980s, not long after the death of Franco. Spanish police and soldiers stood outside public buildings keeping silent watch, automatic rifles at the ready.

One afternoon, pedaling into a very small town, I stopped to buy groceries but saw nothing that indicated a store. Walking along the main street, I came to a doorway with just a dark curtain across it. I could hear voices and decided to go in and ask about a grocery. As I leaned my bike against the wall, I realized I understood nothing of what was being said inside. It wasn't Spanish and I had no idea what it might be. I drew the curtain back to step in and before my foot hit the floor, everyone speaking had switched to Spanish. It turned out that whatever the language, it was a grocery. I bought a small packet of rice along with an onion, a pepper, and a chunk of cheese. When I left the store, everyone inside switched from Spanish back to the language I couldn't identify. It was years before I figured out that must have been Basque, and more years before I'd learned enough to begin to understand the reluctance of many Basques to publicly speak their language.

The point was driven home when, more than twenty years after that grocery experience, I was in the Basque Country studying the language. One Saturday morning, a Basque friend and I were walking in the Old Town section of the southern Basque city of Tolosa, talking as we walked—in Basque. Our conversation was interrupted when a woman coming toward us stepped in our path forcing us to stop. "*Habla en Cristiano*," she said. Speak Christian. Which means speak Spanish.

Partly because of the pressure to use Spanish and French and partly as a result of geography—a land of steep mountains and narrow valleys in which communities had only limited contact with one another—there have been significant local differences in Basque. In the 1860s, French philologist Louis-Lucien Bonaparte produced his map showing eight major dialects of the language that he divided into 25 varieties and 36 sub-varieties.

This linguistic diversity took place in a country approximately the size of Massachusetts. That's if we consider the entire nation—the Basque Autonomous Community, the historic Community of Navarre, and the three provinces under French rule—Lapurdi, Lower Navarre, and Zuberoa. If we consider only the Basque Autonomous Community, those multiple dialects were spoken in a country slightly larger than Delaware. Only in the 1960s was Basque unified with a standard written and spoken version—Batua.

My first chore in translating these medieval poems and songs was thus to bring the older language into contemporary Batua. Many times I couldn't make head nor tail of the poems because of orthography—how words were spelled. Sometimes a poem would be written using French spelling. Sometimes Spanish. Now and again Latin. The same phrase or sentence might appear in dramatically different forms according to the knowledge or tastes of the transcriber. The hissing sound of the *s* as in snake might be rendered as *s*, *z*, or *ç*. The voiced and unvoiced consonants might be reversed—*v* and *f*, *b* and *p*, *d* and *t*, *k* and *g*. The *k* sound might be represented as a *c* or as *que*, the *b* sound as a *v*.

In some cases, it appeared that the transcriber didn't speak Basque and simply put down an idiosyncratic imagined phonetic rendering of the sounds. A single Basque word might appear on the page as two or three words. Or two Basque words might be made into one, the end of the first tacked onto the beginning of the second. An example of this appears in "Çutegon," translated here as "On My Feet." In an early print publication, the first two lines of the poem (which is only one line in our translated version)—I'm on my feet but can't stand still—appeared as "Çutegon / e çinguel deriquegon." A medieval Basque speaker who knew how to read and write French and heard this phrase would have known it was *Çut egon, / eçin gueldiric egon*. In Batua that would be *Zutik egon, / ezin geldirik egon*.

Seeing "Çutegon" for the first time, I remembered my introduction to French as a student in Paris. In greeting, people said something that sounded to me like "sah-vah." It was both a question and an answer. I thought it was one word and spent a lot of time trying to look it up in my little traveler's pocket dictionary, going down the lists of all the words beginning with *sa*. I never found it, though I did learn the words *sauver*, to save; *savoir*, to know; and *savant*, a learned person.

*Savant* opens up another problematic aspect of translation—denotation versus connotation, the dictionary definition of a word versus the ideas or feelings that a word evokes. The dictionary renders savant as scholarly, learned, and clever, three words with quite different connotations for English speakers. Scholarly often implies bookish, perhaps not fully engaged with the demands of daily life, with a narrow specialist's focus. Learned often suggests someone who has thought deeply, who may even exhibit wisdom. And clever, well, a clever person is someone not to be trusted. Clever like a fox, we say. Smart, tricky, deceitful.

In writing this preface to *Forest of Ash*, I've described some of the poems and songs that have come down to us—their subjects and what those subjects reveal to us about medieval Basque life and its link to present Basque experience. I've mentioned scholarly works on medieval Basque literature. And I've addressed a few of the common difficulties translators face when confronting the limits of translation in terms of both linguistic difference and human consciousness. I hope that what I've said here and in the notes accompanying each of the poems will help readers enter the world evoked by the *Forest of Ash*.

David Romtvedt
Buffalo, Wyoming, autumn/udazkena 2023

# Beotibarko kantua / The Song of Beotibar

Beotibar is a small community in the Belauntza municipality east of Tolosa, Gipuzkoa, not far from the border with Navarre. Gipuzkoa was part of the Kingdom of Navarre from 824 CE when the first king, Eneko Aritza, was crowned. In 1200, Castile conquered Gipuzkoa and the region experienced increasing social instability.

A now-famous battle took place at Beotibar in 1321. Once said to have arisen as a result of conflict between Navarre, its French allies, and Castile over access to Gipuzkoan seaports, it was more likely caused by banditry, especially cattle rustling.

Gil Lopez Oñaz, Lord of Larrea and Araban bandit leader, attacked the castle at Gorriti in Navarre. In response, the local governor, Ponz de Mortagne, called up troops to punish the thieves and, according to one rather romantic chronicle, left Iruñea-Pamplona on September 13, leading a force of 60,000 men. Given that there weren't 60,000 people in all of Navarre at the time, it's an unlikely number. The actual figure appears to have been around 450. This smaller force allegedly burned the Gipuzkoan town of Berastegi, including the church which was said by the invaders to have abandoned its religious duties.

On September 19, Mortagne's forces reached the narrow Valley of Beotibar where they were attacked by the troops of Lopez Oñaz. The sixteenth-century historian Esteban Garibai wrote that Lopez Oñaz ordered old wine vats to be filled with stones and thrown from the slopes that flanked the "narrow and rugged" road along which the Navarrese marched. The anonymous author of the *Gran Crónica de Alfonso XI*, a late fourteenth-century account of the reign of Alfonso XI, king of Castile and Leon, estimated that about 10,000 Navarrese soldiers lost their lives, but current estimates based on archival documents show that approximately 30 soldiers died in the battle, including Johan Lopiz Urrotz, a prominent knight and very active Navarrese agent in the fight against bandits. Garibai also notes that Martin Oibar, second lieutenant to the king of Navarre, along with his son "and other knights and nobles" were captured, and some of them were murdered by Gil Lopez Oñaz's men.[1]

According to the sixteenth-century Gipuzkoan writer, diplomat, and political figure Juan Martínez Zaldibia, Lopez Oñaz's victory was widely celebrated and gave rise to one of the oldest songs in Basque literature, the existing fragment of which is included here. Zaldibia himself is the probable composer of "The Song of Beotibar."[2]

Claudio Otaegi's nineteenth-century poem "The Battle of Beotibar" was adapted for music by Lourdes Iriondo and Aire Ahizpe and can be heard on the recording *Nafarroa - La Navarre: Chants et Traditions*. Another version of the poem was recorded by Benito Lertxundi on his 1993 album *Hunkidura Kuttunak II*. Following these musical leads, our translation is rhymed and metered as if it were for a sung version of the poem.

# Beotibarko kantua

Milla vrte ygarota
hura vere videan.
Guipuzcoarroc sartu dira
Gaztelaco echean,
nafarroquin vildu dira
Beotibarren pelean...[3]

# The Song of Beotibar

A thousand years gone by,
the water takes its course.
Gipuzkoa will with Castile lie
by choice, some say by force.
With Navarre gone former ties,
now war our sole recourse.

# Urruxolako guduaren kanta / Song of the Battle of Urruxola

According to Juan Carlos de Guerra in his 1924 book *Los Cantares antiguos del euskera: viejos textos del idioma*, the battle of Urruxola, Gipuzkoa, fought sometime between 1388 and 1401, arose because of conflict over private property boundaries and the use of communal pasture lands. Unable to settle their differences through negotiation, several families, led by the Ganboas of Oñati and the Galarzas of Leintz, agreed to meet in battle on a predetermined day at Urruxola, a hamlet between their two towns. The battle was bloodier than either side expected—three Galarza brothers leading the forces of Leintz were killed, while Pedro Garibai who led Oñati's victorious forces was badly injured. Happy to have won the battle, Garibai was able to ignore the pain of his injuries to both compose and chant a victory song on the field of battle. When told of Garibai's injuries, the father of the Galarza brothers said that his sons' deaths would be worth it if their enemy too died. And that's what happened—Garibai died a few days after the battle, perhaps with his victory song still on his lips. He left behind no heirs to his estate or to his victory.[4]

The fragment we've printed here is from a poem first recorded by Juan Pérez Lazarraga in the late sixteenth century and included in Juan Carlos de Guerra's 1924 *Los Cantares antiguos del euskera*.[5]

# Urruxolako guduaren kanta

Gayçaçenduan lenizanos Urruxolaco lecayoa
sendo cenduan odolori biurtu, jaçu gazayoa.[6]

# Song of the Battle of Urruxola

From Leintz, hot to trot, Urruxola's running dogs.
Not so bold now, blood turned to curds.

# Akondiako kanta /
# Song of Akondia

According to Lope García Salazar in the *Istoria de las bienandanças e fortunas*, published in 1476, Lopez Ganboa, assisted by troops from the Ganboas and the Ibarguens of Durango, laid siege in 1390 to the Unzueta tower in Eibar, Gipuzkoa. Gomez Gonzalez Butron "The Elder" sent his brother Otxoa Perez Butron and his fifteen-year-old son Gonzalo Gomez, along with every available person in the Butron household, to help defend the tower. When the forces from Butron arrived, they engaged Lopez Ganboa's troops just above the tower on the slopes of Mount Akondia, a 748-meter-high mountain also known as Arrikurutz that rises above Eibar. The battle between the troops of Oiñaz and Butron, led by the house of Unzueta, and the troops of Ganboa, led by the house of Ibarguen, ended with the Oiñaz faction victorious. Joanes Ibarguen, Ibarguen family head and captain of Ganboa's troops, died in the battle and was said to have left behind "…cauldrons full of meat and many weapons and all the artillery and mules and other tools."[7]

The short fragment—a single line—that we have of this song was reproduced in *The Ibarguen-Cachopín Chronicle*, a manuscript written between 1558 and 1610 by the son of the city of Laredo's chronicler, García Fernández de Cachopín, with the help of the scribe Juan Iñiguez Ibarguen (Arriolabengoa, 1996). Koldo Mitxelena published this fragment in his 1964 work *Textos arcaicos vascos* (Ancient Basque Texts).

# Akondiako kanta

Acundia lejarr[a]ga lejarbaga.[8]

# Song of Akondia

Akondia, forest of ash, the absent trees.

# Ahetzeko anderearen kanta / The Lady of Ahetze's Song

This is the story of Menauton Urrutia and his wife Domenja. The central theme of the poem is gender violence—the husband's jealousy and mistreatment of his wife. Menauton accuses his wife of being with another man. When she tells him she is innocent of his charge, he grabs her by the hair and drags her along the ground. In the face of her husband's mistrust, Domenja is an outsider in her own home—her heart is far away.

Alluding to the legend of Saint Clare, the second part of the poem follows Domenja as she gets up early to prepare bread for the poor. Leaving home with the basket of bread on her head, she is stopped by her husband who suspects she is going to meet her lover. She tells him to look inside the basket, and when he puts his hand in, the loaves of bread become balls of yarn. Only then does he see that he's made a terrible mistake by mistrusting her and asks her forgiveness. The poem doesn't explain how it is that the miracle of turning bread to balls of yarn proves Domenja was a faithful wife. Nor does it explain how she's to feed the poor with bread turned to yarn. The miracle serves only to awaken the husband to the falsehood of his accusations, to help him see how wrong his violent mistreatment of his wife has been. Among the striking features of the song is the mixing of voices—at one moment it seems to be Menauton who speaks, at another it's Domenja, and sometimes it's an unnamed commentator.

"Ahetzeko anderearen kanta" was published as "Hauzeko anderia" (The Lady of Hauze) in Francisque Michel's 1857 book *Le Pays Basque*. In 1899, Jean de Jaurgain published it in his *Quelques légendes poétiques du pays de Soule* under the title "Ahetzeko anderia" (The Lady of Ahetze). Jaurgain explained that the poem should not be titled "Hauzeko anderia" because a woman from that family never married an Urrutia. Agreeing with Jaurgain that "Hauzeko anderia" was inaccurate, Txomin Peillen noted that whatever Domenja's original family name, she married into the house of Urrutia and so recommended the title "Urrütiako anderea" in his article "Altzürükü Urrutiako leinuaren eresiak XV. mendeko" (Fifteenth Century Ballads of Altzuruku Urrutia) published in 1986 in the Academy of the Basque Language (Euskaltzaindia) magazine *Euskera*.[9]

# Ahetzeko anderearen kanta

Ahetzeko anderea
Urrütian korpützez,
hor dizü bere bürüa
kanpoan da bihotzez.

Nor dü bere maitea
nahi nüke egia.
Jinkoak nahi badü
hiltzea üken dü.

Gure jaun Ürrütia
kexüan beti zira.
Erradazü zertako
ni ez nüzü kanpoko.

Hürrun zite niganik
ez dit zure beharrik,
bazoaza kanpora
neri adar biltzera.

Jauna holako gaüzak
Ahetzeko andereak
ez ditizü ikasi
heen doazü ihesi.

Ele horiek ahoti
jalkitzen zirelarik,
Urrütiak bilhoti
herresta dü ibili.

# The Lady of Ahetze's Song

Next to her Lord Urrutia
lies the Lady of Ahetze,
her head on the pillow,
her heart far away.

Who holds it,
that heart? I'd like
to know. May God
strike him dead.

My Lord Urrutia,
always so uneasy.
And for what?
There's no other.

Get away from me.
I don't need you.
Go, if you're going
to make me the fool.

Sir, the lady
knows nothing
of such things,
flees from them.

These stories, well,
people talk. They say
Urrutia drags her
around by her hair.

Jinkoa zer bizia!
Oi! Jaun Ürrütia.
Ni Ahetzeko etxean
nindagozün bakean.

Hona jin behar nizün
ene sortea züzün,
bihotzmin ükeiteko
zure kexarazteko.

Ogen gabe zü beti
mintzo zitzaist gogorki.
Otoi zure begiak
ütz ditzala kexüak.

Goizean goizik jeikirik
ogi opilak eginik,
Ahetzeko Anderia
lehia dün handia.

Zareta bat bürüan
kanporat jalkitzean,
Musd'Ürrütiak züan
baratü bai bidean.

Nun zabiltza hain goizik
jauregia hüstürik?
Galtatzen dio Ürrütik
begiak oldartürik.

Jauna ikusiko düzü
nahi balin badüzü,
norat orai nabilan,
zareta bat bürüan.

Oh God, such a life!
My Lord Urrutia,
I came to you,
to Ahetze, in peace.

I had to come
to you, it was fate,
to suffer heartache,
suffer your complaints.

Always hard words
no matter my innocence.
May your eyes
one day be opened.

Rising early
to bake bread,
the mistress of Ahetze,
hard at work.

Opening the door,
basket on her head,
Master Urrutia
blocks her way.

Where are you going,
Urrutia asks, leaving
the palace so early?
Threat in his eyes.

My Lord, look
if you want, see
where I'm going,
basket on my head.

Jente eskeleari
emaiteko sokorri,
Madama Ürrütiak
hartü zütüan bideak.

Opilez zarea baitzen
beterik jente prauben.
Ürrütiak zarian
esküa ezarri züan.

Opilak ordü hartan
jin ziren haillilkotan.
Urrütiak berhala
ustez trunpatü zela,

Ehülearen etxera
zoaz bilberaztera.
Jauna ikusten düzü
orai zük badakizü.

Parka izadazüt arren
bekaitz ez nüzü izanen,
emazte on zirela
orai badit nik proba.[10]

I would help those
in need, and with that
Madame Urrutia
stepped away.

A basket of bread
for the poor.
Urrutia thrusts
his hand in.

With that the bread
became balls of yarn—
and Urrutia saw suspicion
had blinded him.

You want something
woven, go to the weaver.
You see, my Lord,
now you know.

Forgive me, please.
No more jealousy.
Of a good wife,
here is the proof.

# Ahetzeko anderearen kanta (bigarren bertsioa) / The Lady of Ahetze's Song (second version)

This version of the Lady of Ahetze's story gives information about Domenja Urrutia's birthplace and family background—her ancestors and her links with various Basque families. In this telling of the story, the focus is not on the Lord of Urrutia's jealousy but on his extramarital affairs and his mistreatment of his wife. And here, it is not the Lady's virtue and honesty that save her but her brother, the Viscount of Etxauz, who comes to his sister's defense and forces the abusive husband Urrutia to flee out a window of his own palace.

Alan Griffin, in his book *La puerta abierta*, holds that this poem is not a second version of "Ahetzeko anderearen kanta." In Griffin's view, it is unlikely that two oral poems with so many differences would have a common origin.[11] So, while we have two poems with the same name, perhaps we should think of them as two chapters in the Lady of Ahetze's life story. This other chapter was collected by Jesus M. Leizaola and appeared in his book *El Refranero vasco antiguo y la poesia euskerica* (Ancient Basque Proverbs and Poetry) published by Ekin in Buenos Aires in 1978.

# Ahetzeko anderearen kanta
# (bigarren bertsioa)

Sorthu nintzan Etxauzian
hazi Garatian Agerrian
eskolatu Baiunian
Madamatü Urrütian.

Altzürükü Urrütia
ala lekhü famatia
enetako ia izan düzü
phenaz hiltzeko lekhia.

Musde Urrütia bilhoa holli
jaun erretorak hortzak zuri;
haiek biek ni narabila
Urrütian eztezari.

Kozinatik kanberala
kanberatik kozinala
hiruetan üngürazi zeitan
bilho adatsa eskietan.

Musde Urrütia etzen lotzen
bere tela mihisetan
araxe nahiago beitzen
amoriaren kapitetan.

A Baigorri, Baigorri maite
nik hilik ere hara nahi nuke
han harriak ere althe nituzke,
[…]

# The Lady of Ahetze's Song (second version)

I was born at Etxauz,
raised at Garatia in Agerria,
sent to school in Baiona,
married off at Urrutia.

Altzürükü Urrutia—
place of renown,
for me, place of
torment and death.

The manor lord is blond
and the abbott has white teeth.
At Urrutia, they treat me
as less than nothing.

From the kitchen to the attic,
the attic to the kitchen,
he dragged me up and down
three times, my hair in his hand.

My Lord can't sleep
between his fine linen sheets.
He prefers the rough woven
canvas of his mistress.

Oh, Baigorri, my Baigorri,
better to be there, even dead,
there with the stones of the earth,
[...]

Etxauzeko bizkundia,
non da zure ohoria,
zure arreba anderia
xangrinez hiltzen ari da.

Etxauzeko bizkundia,
beldürra düzü ahalkia
uzten düzü phenaz hiltzera
zure arreba anderia.

Bizkundiak mithilari
zela bedi zaldi hori!
Erra bedi urzo hori,
jar gitian bide horri.

Bizkondia armatürik,
zaldi urdina zelatürik,
Urrütian sarthü züzün.
Urrutia ezkapi leihotik.[12]

Viscount of Etxauz,
have you no honor—
your sister, broken
hearted, dying.

Viscount of Etxauz—
fear and shame—
leaving your sister
to die in misery.

The viscount tells his groom,
"Saddle my horse
and roast a dove.
We're to the highway."

The viscount, weapons drawn,
rides his ash-colored horse
into Urrutia whose Lord
leaps from the window.

# Bereterretxeren kanta / Bereterretxe's Song

For centuries Navarre was marked by conflict between two noble families—the Agramonts and the Beaumonts. By the mid-fifteenth century, intrigue and bad blood led to an open war. The knight Bereterretxe, a partisan of the Agramont clan, was swept up in the conflict. Bereterretxe's murder was ordered by Luis Beaumont, 1st Count of Lerin and military leader of the Beaumont forces.

In the Andotze Valley of Zuberoa, the night before Easter, Luis Beaumont and three dozen armed men appear at the Larraine tower-house of Bereterretxe. Luis, known for his cruelty and deceit, tells the young knight they are taking him to Maule and that he has nothing to fear. Of course, Bereterretxe knows he has plenty to fear, but, chained and dragged away, he faces death with courage and dignity. On the way to Maule, where he's to be executed, his captors apparently grow impatient and decide to hurry things along. They stop at the Ezpeldoi neighborhood in Etxebar, tie their prisoner to an oak tree, fire two arrows through him, and leave the body either tied to the tree or hanging from it. It's an old story and accounts differ.

Aware of her son's capture, Bereterretxe's mother Marisantz crosses the five peaks of the Bosmendieta mountain range and down to her family's house—Buztanobi—in Lakarri. She asks her younger brother for help. He tells her that if Bereterretxe is alive he will be in Maule. Just as there is no explanation why the murderers couldn't wait for the scheduled execution in Maule, there is no explanation why Marisantz's brother is unable or unwilling to do anything to save his nephew's life. Nor is it explained how he knows the young man has been captured and taken to Maule. One thing all the chronicles agree on is that in this period Navarre was a hotbed of intrigue.

Leaving Buztanobi, Marisantz walks all night—thirty kilometers through the Andotze Valley. Passing Ezpeldoi, she asks about her son. The locals deny any knowledge of his death. In Maule, Luis tells Marisantz that her son is in Ezpeldoi, that she can "go, bring him back to life." Realizing that the people of Ezpeldoi have lied to her, she vows to never forgive them.

The story ends with Margarita of Ezpeldoi washing Bereterretxe's bloody shirts in the nearby river. Some say there's a love story here that explains why Luis stopped in Ezpeldoi to murder Bereterretxe. Others say the laundry scene is only to symbolize the crime Luis has committed.

Bereterretxe's story was transmitted orally through the centuries until Jean Jaurgain published it in 1899 in *Quelques légendes poétiques du pays de Soule*. According to Jaurgain, the song was composed between 1434 and 1449, when Luis Beaumont, 1st Count of Lerin, controlled the castle of Maule on behalf of the King of England. Today, we can witness the unfortunate fate of Bereterretxe through Mikel Laboa's 1964 recording of the poem.

# Bereterretxeren kanta

Haltzak ez dü bihotzik,
ez gaztanberak hezürrik.
Ez nian uste erraiten ziela
aitunen semek gezurrik.

Andozeko ibarra,
ala zer ibar lüzia!
Hiruretan ebaki zaitan
armarik gabe bihotza.

Bereterretxek oheti
neskatuari eztiki:
"abil, eta so egin ezan
gizonik denez ageri."

Neskatuak ber'hala,
ikusi zian bezala
hiru dozena bazabiltzala
borta batetik bestila.

Bereterretxek leihoti
Jaun kuntiari goraintzi:
ehun behi bazereitzola,
beren zezena ondoti.

Jaun kuntiak ber'hala,
traidore batek bezala:
"Bereterrex, haigü bortala:
ützüliren hiz berhala."

# Bereterretxe's Song

Alder has no heart
and cottage cheese no bones.
I wouldn't have believed
noblemen lied.

The Andotze Valley—such
a long valley. Three times
they broke my heart.
Not with weapons.

Bereterretxe, in bed,
whispers to the serving girl,
"Go and look to see
if any men appear."

Quick as she can,
she checks, tells him,
"Three dozen
going door to door."

At the window, Bereterretxe
calls to Count Beaumont—
the bull followed
by his hundred cows.

The Honorable Count—
a lying snake—speaks,
"Come out, Bereterretxe,
you'll be home soon."

"Ama, indazüt atorra
mentüraz sekulakoa!
Bizi denak oroit ükenen dü
bazko gai-erdi ondua."

Heltü nintzan Ligira,
buneta erori lürrera,
buneta erori lürrera
eta eskurik ezin behera.

Heltü nintzan Ezpeldoira,
han haritx bati esteki,
han haritx bati esteki
eta bizia zeitan idoki.

Marisantzen lasterra
bost mendietan behera!
Bi belainez herrestan
sartü da Lakarri-Büstanobila.

"Büstanobi gaztia,
ene anaie maitia,
hitzaz onik ez balinbada,
ene semea joan da".

"Arreba, hago ixilik!
Ez otoi egin nigarrik
hire semea bizi bada,
Mauliala dün joanik."

Marisantzen lasterra
Jaun kuntiaren bortala!
"Ai, ei, eta, jauna,
nun düzie ene seme galanta?"

"Hand me my shirt,
Mother, maybe forever."
The living remember
Easter morning.

I came to Ligi.
My cap fell to the ground,
my cap fell to the ground,
and I couldn't reach down.

I came to Ezpeldoi
where they tied me to an oak,
and there, dead, I was found
where they tied me to an oak.[14]

Marisantz hurrying down
from the Five Peaks,
dragging herself on her knees
to Lakarri-Buztanobi.

"Buztanobi, dear
younger brother,
there is no good way
to say my son is gone."

"Hush, sister,
don't ask this of me.
If your son's alive,
he'll be in Maule."

Marisantz hurries again,
now to the count's door.
"Tell me, sir, where
you've taken my good son?"

"Hik bahiena semerik
Bereterretxez besterik?
Ezpeldoi altian dün hilik;
habil, eraikan bizirik..."

Ezpeldoiko jenteak,
ala sendimentü gabeak!
Hila hain hüllan üken
eta deüsere ez zakienak!

Ezpeldoiko alaba
Margarita deitzen da:
Bereterretxen odoletik
ahürka biltzen ari da.

Ezpeldoiko bukata,
ala bukata ederra!
Bereterretxen atorretarik
hirur dozena ümen da.[13]

"Do you have sons
other than Bereterretxe,
dead above Ezpeldoi?
Go, bring him back to life."

The unfeeling people
of Ezpeldoi—the dead
man so near and they say
they know nothing.

Ezpeldoi's daughter
Margarita, the blood
of Bereterretxe
filling her hands.

Ezpeldoi's laundry—
endless laundry!
Bereterretxe's shirt,
as if it were three dozen.

# Peru Abendañoren edo Aramaioko guduaren kanta / Peru Abendaño's Song or The Battle of Aramaio

"Peru Abendaño's Song," also known as "The Battle of Aramaio," was described in Francisco Mendieta's *Quarta parte de los annales de Vizcaya* (Fourth Part of the History of Bizkaia), a work written in the seventeenth century and first published in 1915. In 1964, the account was republished in Koldo Mitxelena's *Textos arcaicos vascos* (Ancient Basque Texts). The song describes a local conflict arising out of a fifteenth century series of what might be called gang wars, family feuds, or territorial struggles between competing warlords.

In 1443, the king of Castile's first crossbowman Peru Abendaño, Lord of Legutio, along with his family members and the treasurer of Bizkaia, Ochoa Sánchez de Guinea, entered Otxandio in southern Bizkaia and burned the fortresses of the Butron family. The attackers then traveled to Aramaio, six kilometers away in Araba, where they burned twenty houses, fourteen of which belonged to Joanes Mendiola. When told of this, Mendiola and his supporters sought out Abendaño's men at Aramaio, killing four of them. Mendiola then confronted a group of looters, killing their leader about whom we know only his name—Gaxto Apala—a derogatory nickname that might be translated as Low Badness. After being stabbed with a spear, Gaxto Apala was dragged along the ground by the hair until he died. Shades of Achilles at Troy. Intending to burn the body, Mendiola was stopped by a group of women who urged him not to waste time with the dead, to instead help those who were still alive. While it's unclear how Mendiola could simultaneously help the wounded and track down the fleeing attackers, that's what he did. Catching Abendaño's men as they crossed the pass at Izarraga on the way back to Legutio, there was another fight in which Mendiola's supporters defeated the remains of Abendaño's force.

While the story makes no mention of the stolen goods that were the purpose of the raid—cows, sheep, grain—no motive beyond theft is offered. Nor is there mention of any negotiation as to the fate of Abendaño. We know he survived, as he is the speaker in the song. Did he take off running when Mendiola arrived? Did the two noble lords agree there would be no further bloodshed? This is possible, given the medieval penchant to throw away the lives of peasants while treating noble enemies as friends.

What we know is that this epic battle occurred between armies that probably numbered between ten and twenty combatants each, and that Abendaño had regrets. Speaking from the battlefield at the summit of Izarraga, he was horrified by the lifeless bodies at his feet. He mourned the death of Gaxto Apala and that of the other men who fell with him, saying that had he known his raid would end in a bloodbath, he would not have attacked Otxandio or Aramaio. Notwithstanding this expression of regret, Abendaño quickly reverted to his old self when, a few weeks later, he burned down the houses of a number of Mendiola's supporters.

# Peru Abendañoren edo Aramaioko guduaren kanta

Yzarragati gora elcian joeala
Jaun Peru Abendañococ esala:
oñetaco lurrau jauil[t] ycara,
gorpuceco lau araguioc berala.

Oi aldioneri albanegui empara,
barriz enendorque Aramaioco contrara.
Mendiola, yl deustac Gasto Apala,
bere lagunzat beste asco ditubala.[15]

# Peru Abendaño's Song or The Battle of Aramaio

Lord Peru Abendaño
looks down from Izarraga's peak.
"The earth trembles under my feet,"
he says, "and the trembling fills me.

Oh, could I have escaped this,
I'd not have attacked Aramaio,
Mendiola killing Gaxto Apala
and so many who came to help."

# Arrasateko erreketako kanta / Song of the Burning of Arrasate

From 1437 to 1447, there was ongoing fighting between various families and their allies associated with groups from the towns of Oiñaz and Ganboa. Led by the Abendaños on the Ganboa side and by the Butrons and Muxikas on the Oiñaz side, this fighting resulted in the burning of Otxandio in 1437 and 1443, Aramaio and Mungia in 1443, Zumarraga, Azkoitia, and Elgeta in 1446, and Berastegi, Legazpia, and Larrabetzu in 1447.

The conflicts came to a head in 1448 when the Guraia family, aligned with Oiñaz, fought the Bañez (or Ibañez) family, aligned with Ganboa, for the control of Arrasate. The Guraia-Oiñaz group asked for help from various supporters of Gomez Gonzalez of Butron and Muxika. *The Ibarguen-Cachopín Chronicle* of 1558-1610 states that Gomez Gonzalez entered Arrasate "with many people intending to take revenge for what had happened in Aramaio," that is, the burning of the town by Peru Abendaño (Arriolabengoa, 1996). Gomez Gonzalez's appearance caused the Abendaños along with Martin Ruiz of Arteaga and Peru Belez of Gebara to enter the fight in support of the Bañez-Ganboa group. Events quickly spun out of control. Gebara's Peru Belez was also Lord of Oñati, Salinas, and Leintz, so these communities also lent support to the Bañez-Ganboa forces. Other allies of Bañez-Ganboa came from Zarautz, Balda, and Iraeta.

As the Chronicle notes, ". . . all the power of the Ganboans" was brought to bear. Still, it wasn't enough. Seeing it would be impossible to take Arrasate in an open assault, Peru Belez set up a perimeter blockade and ordered that the town be burned. When the defenders fled the fire, he killed them. The dead included the Guraia-Oiñaz supporter Gomez Gonzalez who was murdered along with his son Juan Gonzalez, his nephew Perceval, and twenty-five of his men. On the Bañez-Ganboa side, fifteen men were killed and an unknown number were wounded. The dead and wounded included men from Gebara, Urkizu, and Arteaga.[16] Arrasate was almost completely destroyed by the fires.

The poem begins with a critique of the allies of the Guraia-Oiñaz forces for having entered the battle with insufficient strength. The heroism of the dead, and the cowardice and cruelty of the Bañez-Ganboas, is addressed, as is the extreme cowardice of the Guraia-Oiñaz-aligned Lord of Ozaeta who fled the field leaving his men behind. As is the case with many of these early Basque songs and poems, multiple voices are heard as if we are seeing fragments of separate works that have been conjoined.

# Arrasateko erreketako kanta

Gal didila Untzueta ta Bergara.
Zaldibarrek bere partea debala.
Aramaio, suak erre hazala.
Ta sumi a[..]la Guraiarra,
zeren zeuren jauna ez zentzan enpara.

Gomez handia zan arren,
han zan Presebal bere,
bai Joanikote bere.
Madalenan han ei dautza
biola-tronpeta bage.

Gomizek asko lagunik,
zabal arabarrik,
giputz ondo ederrik,
bizkaitar urduri gogorrik.
Ez diatzo bakarrik,
ze han daz Presebal hilik,
Juanikotegaz lagundurik,
txibuluen ospe bagerik,
ez urrun Malogenik.

Argizarrak urten dau
zeruan goian ostantzean;
Bergararrok hasi dira
trazioe baten asmatzean,
euroen artean dioela:
erre dezagun Mondragoe.
Lasterreon sar gaitezan
kantoeko sartzaikeran,
haen bizarrak ikara zirean
armakaz ezin egien legez ezer

# Song of the Burning of Arrasate

May Untzueta and Bergara disappear
from the earth. Zaldibar, too.
May Aramaio and the Guraians
end a smoking ruin, punishment
for not protecting your lord.

Although Gomez was great,
and Perceval and Joanikote, too,
all lie now in the hermitage
of Madalena, where neither
viola nor trumpet plays.

Gomez and his friends—
the numerous Arabans
and sturdy Gipuzkoans,
the Bizkaians with nerves
of steel. They're not alone—
Perceval, too, died there,
and Joanikote come to his aid
near Malogen, no flute,
no song to their glory.

Hung from the roof
of sky, a star appeared.
The Bergarese plotted
betrayal—let's burn
Arrasate, find the gap,
cross the border now,
moving fast. Beards
trembling, unable to win
an honest victory, even
with superior weaponry,

Ganboarrok su emaitean
hasi dira, ta honegaz urten daude ber'alan
Oñeztar barruangoak
zein erre ez zitezan.
Gomiz Gonsalutx bertan zan,
Beragaz Presebalen kaltean
Joanikok eta beste askok
eudela parte bertan.

Oin harrok zituan luma
Ozaetaco jaun gazteak;
laster baten igaro zan
uraz alde bestean.
ama bereak esan eutsan:
semea, zer dok horrelan?
zaurietan kuradu eta,
ama, nagozu ohera.
Egun behin ur jarruta
Ganboar seme lasterra,
are bere lasterrago
Abendañue Motela.
Eskerrik asko emaiten deutsat
Andra Santa Maiñari:
bera axei zat sartu eta
etxera bidaldu nau ni.[17]

the Ganboans set the fire,
let it burn and walked away.
Trapped inside, the men
of Oiñaz still alive, died.
Gomez Gonzalez was there
and Perceval—his own fault—
and Joaniko[18] and so many more
who had played their part.

You'd think Ozaeta's young
lord wore the winged sandals
of Hermes on his proud feet—
how he crossed the river
in a single great leap.
"What's happened, my son?"
his mother asked.
"Take me to my bed, mother,
and heal my wounds.
Today, Ganboa's quick son,
and the even quicker Abendaño
who stutters, drove me
across the river. I thank
Saint Marina, holy lady
who appeared
and carried me home."

# Errodrigo Zaratekoaren kanta / Rodrigo of Zarate's Song

Between 1448 and 1468, Errodrigo—Rodrigo—Zarate, Lord of Legutio, was involved in a series of conflicts with neighboring nobles. These conflicts reflected decades of ongoing violence that kept Araba and Bizkaia's Arratia Valley in nearly continual turmoil. Bands associated with the Abendaño and Kortazar factions raided, plundered, and committed murders in Markina, Zuia, Zigoitia, and other communities throughout the area.

This poem, recorded in *The Ibarguen-Cachopín Chronicle* of 1558-1610 (Arriolabengoa, 1996), recounts the battle Errodrigo and his allies fought against Juan of Abendaño, Sarmiento of Castile, Asensio of Gebara, and two figures identified by the chroniclers only as Billela and Arteaga— "The good brothers."[19]

Errodrigo, who goes to battle riding a horse adorned with five hundred bells, loses Markina-Zuia and is forced to flee. He later swears fidelity to the lords of Urkizu, agreeing to pay homage to them by "lighting two candles . . . in the tower at Legutio."

# Errodrigo Zaratekoaren kanta

Arma escuduac on dira dardos,
pareric estabe canporacos,
çaratearrac galdu ei dabe Marquia-Çuya çeculaco.

E[rrodrigo] Çarateco, selan xuga[...]a sindean
Jaun Juane Abendañocogas gudua arçen sanean,[20]
bi milla guiçon oi ditus bere lelengo deiean,
lau milla bere baleduque premia letorrenean,
Cortaçarretarrac delanterea, Ibarguendarrac urrean,
Gastelan Sarmientuarric asco, es pareric arean,
Jaun Asençio Guebaraco ganean darda ordean,
Billela ta Arteaga, anage onac urrean,
saldusunac on[...]rrenean,
onac arin, gog[oa] sendo, arerioaen asean.

Errodrigo Çarateco saldi urdinaen ganean,
bosteun caxcabel urregorrisco saldiac idurenean,
carrerea laster eroean Erbitegui ganean,
arerioac ur jarraica arre bearen semea,
ona chipi, orpo laster, Abendanochea.

—Arren, echosu orain osaba, bixeoc justa gaitean.
—Echi eguidac orailloba, gau bixiric noean,
neure biçian enoaque Urquiçuren contrean,
omenaje eguingo joat biçia dodan artean,
bela vic sar naxaitec Billa Realgo torrean.[21]

# Rodrigo of Zarate's Song

Unable to match the better weapons
of their invaders, their shields and spears,
Zarate's force lost Markina-Zuia for good.

When Juan Abendaño appeared, Rodrigo
of Zarate fled like greased lightning,
running from the two thousand men Abendaño
had called. Four thousand more would come
if he needed them. Kortazar's troops up front,
Ibarguen's close behind, Sarmiento's Castilians,
fighters beyond compare, Asensio of Gebara
leading the archers. Finally, the good brothers
Billela and Arteaga with their mounted knights—
capable, quick, strong in pursuit of the enemy.

Rodrigo, riding his blue roan,
five hundred burnished gold bells around its neck,
racing wildly above Erbitegi, the enemy after
his sister's son, the one who was
an Abendaño, stealthy and quick.

Please, Uncle, stand, we'll fight together.
Leave, nephew, now. If at nightfall I'm still alive,
I'll never again take up arms against Urkizu,
I'll remain their faithful servant as long as I live,
lighting two candles as pledge in the tower at Legutio.

# Sanda Ilia / Saint Elijah

Crossing the San Adrian Pass near Oñati, a group led by Santxo Gartzia Garibai met a muleteer from Hernani named Joanes Zaar—Old John—and asked him to give them some of the wine he was hauling. Old John refused, so they took all the wine along with his money. There is no explanation in the poem for the theft, but the French writer Francisque Michel in his 1857 book *Le Pays Basque* tells us that miquelets—irregular Valencian and Catalan troops who moonlighted as highwaymen—came regularly to the Basque Country where they lived under the protection of Santxo Gartzia.[22]

Old John, hence, was robbed by a group of semi-professional thieves who were protected by a powerful local figure. Unafraid, the muleteer went to the Brotherhood of Gipuzkoa's chief magistrate who sent his deputy Mendoza, along with several men, to investigate. Warned that Mendoza was coming, Santxo Gartzia and his fellow thieves fled to the San Elías cave (the cave of Saint Elijah the Prophet—Elias in Greek) on the left bank of Araotz Creek. Mendoza's men surrounded the cave entrance and laid siege. The magistrate then sent a shipment of wine to help provision his deputies, but this was stolen by supporters of Santxo Gartzia and brought to the fugitives via a back entrance to the cave a kilometer away from where Mendoza's men waited unaware of the cave's back entrance and equally unaware that the fugitives sat eating and drinking while casually planning their escape—an escape that would be carried out with the aid of a servant named Zalagarda.

The late medieval Basque of the poem tells us that the entry to Saint Elijah's cave was filled with *zizar*—*txitxar* in contemporary Basque, a word that appears to derive from Spanish *chicharra* or *chicharro*. *Chicharra* is a variant of *cigarra*—cicada. If this is the meaning of *txitxar*, it suggests that Mendoza and the other deputies brought buckets of cicadas and threw them into the cave. The other possibility is *chicharro*—what's left when butter or pork fat melts. If it's this, Mendoza's group laid a fat-fueled fire to smoke the fugitives out. The fire motif may derive from the fact that the Hebrew prophet Elijah ascended to heaven in a chariot of fire.

Another clue as to what happened at the cave entrance lies in the word *zendal*—which may be a borrowing from the Spanish *cendal*, one of the meanings of which is the barbs of a feather. In conjunction with the burning pork fat or butter, this suggests flaming arrows and is the meaning given by Francisque Michel who tells us that the brotherhood's men, tired of waiting, fired arrows tipped with burning lard into the cave entrance to drive the fugitives out.

But in the poem it is Mendoza's men who run away, eyes filled with tears, meaning that it was Santxo Gartzia's miquelets who were filling the air with flaming arrows fired from inside the cave. All this rests on the shaky base of the word *zendal* and its possible meaning of a feather's barbs.

Whatever really happened during the siege, the officers of the law left with no arrests made. At this point in the text they are described—for the first time—as being *Lazkaotarrak*, people from the town of Lazkao. The speaker implies Santxo Gartzia's miquelets chased Mendoza's men from the front of the cave. But this can't be true as the thieves had fled out the back way and left the deputies laying siege at the entrance to an empty cave. And if Mendoza's men were really from Lazkao, why are they described as going to an inn rather than home to keep watch through the night? One is inclined to think we're reading only a fragment of the original text.

Still, with its joking tone, its focus on food and drink (a favorite of the Basques), its allusions to the ancient prophet Elijah, and its use of puns, the poem presents a nuanced scene. Take the puns—Santxo Gartzia and his band were associated with the Oiñaz and so could be called *Oñaztarrak*, *Oiñaztarrak*, *Oiñazkarrak* or *Oin azkarrak*, words that mean fleet of foot, and therefore men who could escape capture. The helpful servant Zalagarda's name, which in contemporary Spanish means an ambush, trap, ruse, row, or noisy quarrel, is likely derived from the Old French *eschargarde*, a variant of *eschargaite*—which means a guard patrol. So, while ambush is the contemporary translation of *zalagarda*, guard patrol seems the more likely sense of the word here as the servant Zalagarda appears at the back entrance to the cave.

Prior to Francisque Michel's publication of and comments on the poem in *Le Pays Basque*, Pedro del Puerto printed the poem in 1588 with notes explaining the theft, manhunt, and escape.[23] In 1850 these notes were included in Rafael Floranes's epilogue to Lope de Isasti's *Compendio historial*.[24]

# Sanda Ilia

Ala Zalagarda
Zalagarda mala
Zalagarda gaisto
Oñaztarra oondaco
ardao zuri ardao Madrigalgoa,
ardao zuría Mendoza gana doa,
alabana Sandayli gogoa,
Zalagarda Sandaylira doa.

Sanda iliac atrac ditu zizarrez
nola zizarrez da ala zendalez
Hermandadea arcandoa negarrez
Anso Garcia é gasteluori emunez
ec envinda estiquicha esan ez
Lascavarroen y esataco lastorra
Lascavarroc ostatuan onela:
"Gavaz ere urtunica obela
argui izarroc ditugula candela
ostatuan guera diro igu emenda."[25]

# Saint Elijah

Oh, Zalagarda,
vile Zalagarda,
deceitful Zalagarda,
with the white wine
the fleet-footed Oñaz
men stole, the Madrigal
wine meant for Mendoza.
Ah, well, the prophet Elijah,
his will be done, Zalagarda
at the back of the cave.

At the front entrance, lard
and feathers, flaming arrows.
Santxo Gartzia doesn't waver,
speaks no conciliatory words.
The men of the brotherhood,
eyes burning, retreat to the inn
at Lazkao. "We'll keep watch
this night, the stars for light.
In the meantime, we wait.
Innkeeper! Bring us dinner!"

# Juana, Muxikako eta Butroeko alabaren kanta / The Song of Juana, daughter of Muxika and Butron

Juana's story, which is told here in the context of the ongoing conflicts between the Oiñaz and Ganboa families and communities, links personal history to Basque politics of the day.

Gomez Gonzalez, Lord of Muxika and Butron, and an Oiñaz, had promised his daughter Juana in marriage to Martin Ruiz, Lord of Olaso, and a Ganboa. But before Juana and Martin could marry, Gomez Gonzalez was killed in the burning of Arrasate where the two families and their allies fought. While Martin was an enemy Ganboa, it is said that the younger man tried to help his future Oiñaz father-in-law escape the fires.

After the death of Gomez Gonzalez, his wife and son tried to stop Juana's marriage to Martin. In her song, Juana tells her mother that her father's death is not cause for her to lose her right to marry as she wishes and as her father agreed. In the end, her marriage to Martin was celebrated on January 18, 1450, making her the Lady of Olaso.

While Juana and Martin are said to have married for love, they may also have seen their alliance as one that could build a bridge between the warring factions. Juana's mother and brother, on the other hand, appear to have been concerned about the passage of Oiñaz influence and property into the hands of the Ganboas. If this was their concern, it was a mistaken one, as Basque women had the right to own, administer, and inherit property before and after marriage as well as when they were widowed. Perhaps the mother and brother's real concern was that with her marriage, Juana's voice would become more influential than their own in the management of both Oiñaz and Ganboa resources and wealth.

As with many Basque works of the period, this fragment has come to us through the genealogy descent of Juan Alonso of Muxika and Butron as it appears in the 1834 publication *Memorial histórico español: Colección de documentos, opúsculos y antigüedades que publica la Real Academia de la Historia*.[26]

# Juana, Muxikako eta Butroeko alabaren kanta

Verba orren, verba gacia
verba orri naz ez daquiola valia
dardoac eguin arren vere aldia
Olaso da ene egoteco aulquia.[27]

# The Song of Juana, daughter of Muxika and Butron

These words, hard words,
mean nothing—words I've heard.
Although the arrow has flown,
at Olaso, by right, I am the throne.

# Ozaetako Santxaren edo Martin Bañezen kanta /
# Santxa of Ozaeta's or Martin Bañez's Song

Collected by Esteban Garibai in his *Compendio historial de las Chronicas y Universal Historia de todos los Reynos d'España* of 1571 and later in the *Memorial histórico español: Colección de documentos, opúsculos y antigüedades que publica la Real Academia de la Historia* of 1834, this poem is an *eresi*—elegy—offered by Santxa Otxoa of Ozaeta, Lady of Mendixur and Maturana in Araba, on the death of her husband, Martin Bañez de Artazubiaga.[28]

For their part in the 1448 burning of Arrasate, Martin and seven others were condemned to death by the king of Castile. Because the eight were convicted in absentia, the victims' relatives to the fourth degree were empowered to personally carry out the death sentences. To the fourth degree included parents, grandparents, great-grandparents, great-great-grandparents, children, grandchildren, great-grandchildren, great-great-grandchildren, brothers, sisters, husbands, wives, aunts, great-aunts, uncles, great-uncles, nieces, great-nieces, nephews, great-nephews, first cousins, and the children of first cousins. It was a lot of potential executioners.

In May of 1464, sixteen years after their conviction, Martin Bañez and Juan Ibañez of Barrutia left Arrasate for Santa Ageda. At the Ibarreta forge, before reaching Garagartza, Martin was killed by six Oiñaz supporters including Juan Alonso of Muxika, who was the son of Gomez Gonzalez of Butron; Otxoa of Urruxola, who was the Lord of Aramaio's brother; and Juan Ortiz, also of Urruxola.[29]

The killers either didn't know or ignored the fact that, in 1461, King Enrique IV had suspended the death sentences of those who'd been found guilty of the burning of Arrasate. Consequently, Martin's killers were convicted of murder and two were executed—Juan Ortiz in 1470 at Arrasate and Otxoa in 1477 at Bilbao.[30]

The first two lines of the elegy use a formulaic phrase common in the medieval Basque epic and seen in this collection previously in "Peru Abendaño's Song" as well as here:

> Oñetaco lurrau jabilt icara,
> lau haragioc vere an verala, . . .

A literal version of this might read "The earth at my feet quakes (or trembles, or is terrified). And like that, so do my four limbs" (the four limbs indicated by *lau haragioc*—the four fleshes). We've rendered this as "The earth trembles under my feet / and the trembling fills me." Such trembling is not surprising given that it is Martin's widow Santxa expressing her desire for revenge, her vow to burn Aramaio to the ground. There will be no forgiveness from Santxa Otxoa. It's a different attitude from that of the other lady of Butron, Juana Gomez Gonzalez, who against the wishes of her mother and brother married the Ganboa leader Martin Ruiz, Lord of Olaso, despite his having taken part in the burning of Arrasate where Juana's father was killed.

This fragment, also known as "Martin Bañez's Song," was likely written in 1464. Bañez is sometimes spelled with an initial *I* (or *Y*) as in the fragment "Martin Ibañez Labiero's Tombstone" that appears next in this collection. As is the case with most of the poems and songs of the period, the author is unknown.

# Ozaetako Santxaren edo Martin Bañezen kanta

Oñetaco lurrau jabilt icara,
lau haragioc vere an verala,
Martin Bañez Ybarretan il dala.
Artuco dot escu batean guecia,
bestean çuci yraxeguia,
erreco dot Aramayo guztia.[31]

# Santxa of Ozaeta's or Martin Bañez's Song

The earth trembles under my feet
and the trembling fills me.
In Ibarreta, Martin Bañez is dead.
With an arrow in one hand
and a blazing torch in the other,
I'll burn Aramaio to the ground.

# Martin Ibañez Labierokoaren hilartitza /
# Martin Ibañez Labiero's Tombstone

*The Ibarguen-Cachopín Chronicle* of 1558 to 1610 (Arriolabengoa, 1996) records many deaths in battles fought throughout the medieval period between local Bizkaian ruling families and larger regional and incipient national entities.[32] Often such fighting reflected local resistance to the rule of the Castilian king and his allies, including the representatives of the Lordship of Bizkaia.

During this period, organizations known as *hermandadeak* (brotherhoods) were formed as trade and community-based groups similar to contemporary labor unions. *Hermandadeak* supported police forces that, operating largely outside the control of the Castilian crown or the Lordship of Bizkaia, apprehended and tried criminal suspects.

One of the victims of the local conflicts and the justice meted out by the *hermandadeak* was Martin Ibañez (also identified as Yuanes or Bañez) Labiero. Ibañez served as an *alcalde*—a local judge—but it's unclear exactly what this position entailed. Some sources state that he was an *alcalde de fuero*—a judge of Bizkaia—while others state that he was an *alcalde de hermandad*, a judge associated with one of the brotherhoods.

Sources from the period agree that Ibañez was murdered in 1393 or 94, and that his killers added the third line of the epitaph that appeared on his gravestone.

The portion of the epitaph not written by his killers names Ibañez as a *zalduna*, a word that means one who went on horseback and is often translated as knight, though in late fourteenth century Basque, *zalduna*—one who has a horse—was also used as a term of broad respect for men who were not necessarily knights.

# Martin Ibañez Labierokoaren hilartitza

Marti Yuanes, Labieruco çalduna,
Vizcayco consejua ta çençuna,
nor ete çan çuri losa ygorrosi eguiçuna?[33]

# Martin Ibañez Labiero's Tombstone

Martin Ibañez, noble gentleman of Labiero,
wise voice of the Bizkaian Council,
who can have humiliated you so?

# Salinasko kontea preso sartu zuteneko kanta / The Song of Those Who Captured the Count of Salinas

First reproduced in *The Ibarguen-Cachopín Chronicle* of 1558-1610 (Arriolabengoa, 1996), this is yet another of the early Basque fragments that enlarges our understanding of Basque power struggles during the fourteenth and fifteenth centuries.

In 1470, King Enrique IV of Castile, acting as Lord of Bizkaia, charged Pedro Fernández de Velasco, Count of Haro, with ending the conflicts that had roiled Bizkaia for more than a hundred years. The king's real aim, though, was not peace but the expansion of Castile's power over the Lordship of Bizkaia.

Attempts to quell disorder only served to trigger alliances among formerly competing local leaders. In Mungia in 1471, Enrique's troops—led by his proxy Pedro Fernández de Velasco and by Pedro's brothers Luis and Sancho, along with Diego Pérez Sarmiento, Count of Salinas, Álvaro de Cartagena, and other Castilian knights—faced troops of the combined local bands led by Juan Alonso Muxika and Pedro Abendaño. With the assistance of Pedro Manrique de Lara, Count of Trebiño, the army of the momentarily unified bands defeated King Enrique's allies. The king's lead officer, Fernández de Velasco, fled the field. Others were not so lucky. Álvaro de Cartagena and a number of the Castilians died, while Diego Pérez Sarmiento, Count of Salinas, was captured and imprisoned in Bilbao. Following this defeat, Enrique IV withdrew his troops from Bizkaia.[34]

The phrase *ser ete dau amoradu guexoaje* could be referring to hypothetical love affairs the count would no longer enjoy or to the more general loss of the pleasures of life.

The comedic mocking first line of the poem—*lelori lelo saraileloa*—might be read as vocables—tra-la-la-la-la—with no particular meaning. But *lelo* in contemporary Basque means a refrain, a chant, a tiring line someone repeats endlessly. Another current meaning is a person who is foolish or mentally incompetent. We've allowed this leakage to influence the translation.

Whether it is just sound or is tied to the idea of the poem, the first line was one of the commonly used formulaic openings in medieval Basque poetry, seen also in "Lelo's Song" and "Perutxo's Song," both from 1536, and in Bernart Etxepare's poem "Sautrela" collected in his 1545 work *Linguae Vasconum Primitiae*.

# Salinasko kontea preso sartu zuteneko kanta

Lelori lelo saraileloa,
Bilbaon catigu dago Salinasgoa,
calea bera burua baxu daroa
ser ete dau amoradu guexoa[c]?[35]

# The Song of Those Who Captured the Count of Salinas

Sing song along a song tra-la-la-la-lau,
the Count of Salinas a prisoner in Bilbao.
Shuffling down the street, eyes to the ground,
what will become of the loves he once found?

# Domenjon de Andiaren kantua / Domenjon Andia's Song

In the late fourteenth century, in response to the violence of the lords of Oiñaz and Ganboa, who were known as the Ahaide Nagusiak—Ruling Brotherhood—Basque communities created city leagues for mutual aid and protection. In 1397, the General Assembly of Gipuzkoa was founded in an effort to build democratic institutions in response to widespread violence and social disorder. Each community in Gipuzkoa was represented and each was given equal voting rights.

In 1410, thirteen years after the Assembly's founding, Domenjon Gonzalez Andia was born in Tolosa, Gipuzkoa. After studying law in several universities, he served as a diplomatic aide in the courts of Castile and Aragon and later in France and England. In 1456, he returned to Gipuzkoa and was appointed "faithful clerk"—secretary—of the General Assembly. In this role, he led the Brotherhood of Gipuzkoa in its 1457 military actions against the Ahaide Nagusiak. The stone tower-houses of the lords of Oiñaz and Ganboa were destroyed, and the lords themselves were dispossessed and exiled, marking the end of a hundred years of ongoing war.

In 1463, Domenjon played a key role in the creation and formation of the Gipuzkoan Aldundi and Batzar—the region's governing body and representative assembly. With their increasing power, these institutions helped to end violence and bring forward democracy, laying the foundation for the political system that governed Gipuzkoa into the nineteenth century.

Appointed chief magistrate of Gipuzkoa, Domenjon promoted the 1474 reciprocal compensation agreement with England, granting English and Gipuzkoan maritime traders financial compensation against losses from piracy. In 1482, he helped to conclude a treaty allowing nearly duty-free trade between Gipuzkoa and England.

It's ironic that for his activities advancing peace, prosperity, and a more egalitarian, representative political system in a time when government was little more than gang rule, Domenjon Gonzalez Andia was called by his contemporaries *Gipuzkoako erregea*—the king of Gipuzkoa.

He died in Zumaia, Gipuzkoa, on November 18, 1489 while attending a meeting of the General Assembly. His body was taken immediately to Tolosa where he was buried the next day. He was survived by his wife Catarina Tapia and his four children.

The four-line fragment we have recalls his activities as both peacemaker and warrior—the apple and the sword.

# Domenjon de Andiaren kantua

Sagarra eder gezatea,
gerriyan ere ezpatea
Domenjon de Andia,
Gipuzkoako erregia.[36]

# Domenjon Andia's Song

Both an apple, sweet bite,
and a sword worn at his side—
Domenjon Andia,
the king of Gipuzkoa.

# Juan Lazkanoren kanta / Juan Lazkano's Song

In 1467, Juan Lopez Lazkano, nicknamed Beltzarana—the dark-haired, dark-skinned, or simply dark one—succeeded his father as Lord of Lazkano in Gipuzkoa and of the Arana Valley in Araba, making him head of one of the most influential families of the Oiñaz clan.

In 1474, when King Enrique IV of Castile died without a clear heir, civil war broke out between supporters of the two claimants to the throne—Enrique's half-sister, Isabel of Castile, and his daughter Juana, Queen of Portugal, who was known as La Beltraneja because she was popularly believed to be the daughter not of Enrique (rumored to be impotent) but of Beltran de la Cueva, First Duke of Alburquerque. Bizkaia and Gipuzkoa, including Beltran, the supposed father of Juana, supported Isabel, while Louis XI, King of France, supported Juana, sending 40,000 troops to besiege Hondarribia.

The defense of the walled town was carried out by Juan Lazkano with 1,000 men. The defenders erected bastions and dug trenches and moats. Using gunfire, they stopped the French at a distance of 3,000 paces, forcing them to begin digging a trench to the town. After nine days, the French retreated to Bayonne where they were greeted with scorn. Learning of the failure, the French king ordered the troops with new leaders back to Hondarribia. The second siege lasted two months, with trenches so close that soldiers on both sides were said to have thrown stones at each other with their bare hands.

The second, longer siege gave Juan Lazkano time to use the power of levies, known in Basque as *abizena deitu*—to call the surname—in order to organize popular militias. These directly engaged the French, who finally abandoned the fight and withdrew.[37]

# Juan Lazkanoren kanta

Juan de Lazcano beltzarana,
Guipuzcoaco capitana,
franzez osteac jaquingo du
ura Ondarrabian zana.[38]

# Juan Lazkano's Song

Juan Lazkano—the dark one,
the one the French army faced
in Hondarribia, the Gipuzkoan
captain they'll long remember.

# Bretainiako kanta / The Song of Brittany

In 1626, the Gipuzkoan Diego Vélez de Idiáquez wrote a letter to Diego de Silva y Mendoza, Count of Salinas, a noted political figure, amateur poet, and patron of writers. While the principal business of Diego Vélez's letter was to ask a favor, he also intended to show his awareness of the count's literary interest and family lineage, and to this end he asked his chaplain in the Alzolaras Valley to include with his letter a poem written by his father Sant Juan Pérez de Idiáquez.

In this poem dedicated to the Count of Salinas, Diego Vélez recounted what he said was his father's eyewitness account of an armed expedition to Brittany led by an earlier Count of Salinas. The poem included details about the embarkation of troops from the port of Pasaia (Gipuzkoa), the various large and small ships in the armada, the priests in procession, and the young women kneeling and praying to God that their beloved Count of Salinas return victorious. It's a vivid poem, but there's no historical record of an expedition under the command of a count of Salinas in the sixteenth century, so it's unlikely that Sant Juan Pérez witnessed such an event.

There is a record of a 1490 expedition of 1,000 men sent by the kings of Castile and Aragon under the command of an even earlier Count of Salinas, Pedro Gómez Sarmiento, to help Princess Ana, Duchess of Brittany, in her opposition to the king of France. This expedition of Castilians, Aragonese, English, and Basques did not achieve its objectives, and while this earlier Count of Salinas returned home safely in October 1490, he did not return victorious.[39]

The half poem stands as a fine example of both the possibilities and limits of literature as a vehicle for historical memory.

# Bretainiako kanta

Salinasgoa Conde
guztien da jabe,
Guipuzcoa herrian
on guztien burua.

Guztioec digoe
borondatez seguicen
Gamboarraquin
Oñaztarroc conforme
Vizcaitican vere
acompañacen debe
Bretoe gaiztoen
becatuac castigacen.

Conde andiorrec
juntaduditu laster
Donostiaco yrian
Passagen embarcatu
onci andiac chipiaquin
flota andia atera
Franciaren vistan
ciudadea dirudi.

Donostiaco murruan
islaren goyenean
abbade guztiacdaode procisioan
mila bendicio
egozten digoela.

Donzella guztiac
daode belaurico
Jaungoicoa debeela

# The Song of Brittany

The Count of Salinas,
master of all things,
lord of all that is
good in Gipuzkoa.

Freely,
we follow him
with the Ganboas,
the Oiñaz,
and the Bizkaians,
to punish
the sins
of Brittany.

In Donostia
the great count
quickly gathered his force,
setting sail from Pasaia
with ships of every size.
Coming into view
in France, the fleet
seemed a vast city.

From Donostia's walls
on the island's crest,
the priests in procession,
the thousand blessings
sent with the troops.

The young maidens
on their knees
speaking to God,

herreguten
deguiola eman
conde laztanari
vitoria andia
gaiztoen contra.

Vicicea debala
onrarequin seguru
Bretaña guztia
vencituric datorren
conde galantori.

Guipuzcoa herrira
non yçango baita
beti becela buru
nobleza guztiaren
aniz estimatua.

Pobluaren onrra
danac becela
guztiac daduzca
vere aguintean.
Guztioc dioe
amar vider amen.[40]

praying
that the beloved
count be granted
a great victory
over the evil enemy,

that the noble count
live long
and be honored,
victorious
over Brittany,

that he return
to Gipuzkoa where
he will stand
always at our head,
respected by all,

honored by the people
as one of their own,
holding us all
in his power,
everyone saying amen,
ten times, amen.

# Milia Lasturkoren eresia /
# The Elegy for Milia of Lastur

"The Elegy for Milia of Lastur" offers entry into several aspects of medieval Basque life and literature. First, there is the fact that elegies were sung by women, emphasizing women's roles as literary writers and performers. Second, the elegy's form, in which two speakers address and respond to one another, is reminiscent of the improvised sung poetry competitions that take place throughout the Basque Country today, suggesting that the medieval elegies may have also included improvisation. A third revealing feature has to do with language and social class. The elegies were written in Basque, the language of people with lower status in the hierarchy of power; while legal documents, proclamations from rulers, church materials, and poetry regarded to have literary value were written almost entirely in Latin, Spanish, and French. Finally, elegies often included accusations and criticisms made by one party against the other as well as references to pre-Christian forces. This resulted in the elegies being officially prohibited by both ecclesiastical and civil authorities. Of course, it's possible that bans on the form had a simpler source in the church's ongoing attempts to limit the voices of women in the public sphere.

"The Elegy for Milia of Lastur" tells of Milia's marriage to Peru Gartzia and her subsequent removal to Arrasate (Mondragón) where she dies in childbirth. Milia's unnamed sister accuses Peru of bad faith—with his wife Milia not yet cold in her grave, Peru is preparing to marry Marina Arrazola. Emphasizing that Peru has behaved dishonorably—that the marriage to Marina is what Peru wanted all along—Milia's sister implies that

Peru and Marina were having an affair. The sister demands that Milia's body be brought home to her grieving parents in Lastur.

At this point Peru Gartzia's sister Santxa Ortiz speaks, defending her brother's honor. Peru has done no wrong; Milia died by God's will alone. Santxa claims Peru is a "Guiçon chipi sotil(a)." *Chipi* would now be *txiki*, meaning small, immature, a child, or young. And, depending on context, *sotil* can mean subtle, astute, prudent, careful, sturdy, good-looking, polite, dapper, neat, elegant, thin, insubstantial, light, faint, tame, or mild. So while we've translated "Guiçon chipi sotil(a)" as a man "of no guile" who would not be deceitful, the line could possibly mean that although Peru was short, he was a handsome man. We assumed it more likely that Santxa would defend her brother's integrity rather than joke about his appearance. Santxa emphasizes that Peru gave Milia a big house with a lot of keys—that is, a lot of money—and that marriage to Peru brought respect and honor to Milia.

Here Milia's sister says again that the Lady of Lastur was wronged. The rafters supporting the vault of heaven have collapsed, striking Lastur's tallest tower and ruining the lives of the lord and lady. Imploring heaven to return the dead woman, Milia's sister adds that she hates the people of Mondragón who have wronged the women of Gipuzkoa.

"The Elegy for Milia of Lastur" was passed down orally until 1854 when Esteban Garibai included it in his memoirs *Los siete libros de la progenie y parentela de los hijos de Estevan de Garibay* (The Seven Books of the Progeny and Kinship of the Sons of Esteban Garibay), published by Pascual Gayangos. In 1992, Benito Lertxundi, inspired by Josquin des Prez's melody for "Mille Regretz," included a song based on Milia's story on his album *Hitaz Oroit*.

# Milia Lasturkoren eresia

[Miliaren ahizpak:]
Cer ete da andra erdiaen çauria?
Sagar errea, eta ardoa gorria.
Alabaya, contrariomda Milia:
azpian lur oça gañean arria.
Lastur-era bear doçu, Milia.
Ayta jaunac eresten dau elia,
ama andreac apaynquetan obia.
Ara bear doçu, Milia,
lausi da cerurean arria,
aurquitu dau Lastur-en torre barria,
edegui dio almeneari erdia.
Lastur-era bear doçu, Milia.
Arren, ene andra Milia Lastur-co,
Peru Garciac eguin deuscu laburto:
eguin dau andra Marina Arraçolaco.
Ezcon bequio, bere idea dauco.

[Peru Garziaren arrebak:]
Eç dauco Peru Garciac bearric
ain ga[c] andia apucadua gatic,
ceruetaco mandatua içanic,
andrarioc ala cumpli jasoric.
Guiçon chipi sotil baten andra çan,
ate arte çabalean oy çan,
guilça porra andiaen jabe çan,
onrra andi asco cumplidu jacan.

[Miliaren ahizpak:]
Arren ene andra Milia Lastur-co,
mandatariac eguin deust gaxtoto.
Cerurean jausi da abea,

# The Elegy for Milia of Lastur

*Milia's sister speaks:*
What follows the pain of giving birth?
Baked apple and rosé wine.
Not so for Milia, cold earth
below, gravestone above.
Come home to Lastur, Milia,
your worthy father is milking the cows
while your good mother prepares your tomb.
You must return, Milia.
A stone from the sky
has landed on Lastur's new tower,
taking out half the battlements.
You must return to Lastur, Milia—
please, My Lady of Lastur,
Peru Gartzia has belittled us,
has married Marina Arrazola.
It's what he wanted all along.

*Peru Gartzia's sister speaks:*
It's not Peru Gartzia
who's to blame for such pain.
Heaven above decides
while we women fulfill our duties.
Married to a man of no guile,
she stood in the wide portico,
mistress of the keys,
much honored.

*Milia's sister speaks:*
To My Lady Milia of Lastur,
the messenger brought bad news.
The rafters holding heaven's roof

jo dau Lastur-co torre gorea,
eroan ditu ango jauna eta andrea,
bata leen, guero bestea.
Bidaldu dogu ceruetara cartea:
arren diguela gure andrea.
Mondr[a]goeri artu deusat gorroto,
Guipuç andraoc artu ditu gaxtoto:
Iturrioç calean andra Maria Balda-co,
Arte calean andra Ojanda Gabiola-co,
errebalean andra Milia Lastur-co.[41]

have fallen on Lastur's tallest tower,
carrying off the lord and lady,
first one, then the other.
We've sent a letter to heaven
that our lady be returned to us.
As for Mondragón, I hate it,
the pain it's brought the women of Gipuzkoa—
on Iturriotz Street, Lady Maria of Balda,
on Arte Street, Lady Otxanda of Gabiola,
and on the outskirts, Lady Milia of Lastur.

# Jançu janto dego de garcigorreta / You Eat, We'll Eat, the Freeloaders' Ball

Spanish musicologist Juan José Rey Marcos—Pepe Rey—describes "You Eat, We'll Eat, the Freeloaders' Ball" as a *zaloma*—*saloma* in Spanish, sea shanty in English. In the days of ships under oar, the galley captain would chant or sing a line and the oarsmen would repeat, using the rhythm to help synchronize their strokes for greater power and efficiency. The rhythmic lines of a *zaloma* often included improvisation—the captain making up phrases that would, through humor or surprise, help make the rowing less onerous. Another characteristic of the *zaloma* was linguistic mixing. A *zaloma* didn't have to make sense or tell a coherent story. It had to keep the oarsmen together, keep their action unified and their minds occupied so as to help them go on through boredom and exhaustion.

While "You Eat, We'll Eat, the Freeloaders' Ball" is an anonymous work, it was probably written—or at least transcribed—around 1500. Along with three other songs that contain Basque words and phrases, it's included in the *Cancionero de Palacio de los siglos XV y XVI* (The Palace Songbook of the 15th and 16th Centuries). This manuscript, published by the composer and musicologist Francisco Asenjo Barbieri in 1890, contains 458 songs dating from the last third of the fifteenth century to the beginning of the sixteenth century.

Number 431 in the *Cancionero de Palacio*, "You Eat, We'll Eat, the Freeloaders' Ball," has been interpreted by scholars and translators in many different ways. Barbieri said he could not satisfactorily interpret the piece.

Cellist and music scholar Igor Saenz Abarzuza writes in his article "Jançu Janto y el acto creativo de la traducción paneresca como per-versión" that the song includes elements any Basque speaker would recognize as Basque, while noting that the phrases must have been transcribed by a non-Basque speaker. Pepe Rey suggests that the transcriber was Alonso Perez d'Alba, the late-fifteenth and early-sixteenth-century Spanish composer whose work is included in the *Cancionero de Palacio* and who was a singer at the court of Queen Isabella. While some researchers believe "You Eat, We'll Eat, the Freeloaders' Ball" mixed Spanish and Basque, the twentieth-century Basque political leader and literary scholar Jesus M. Leizaola held that the song was entirely in Basque while agreeing that it was transcribed by a non-Basque speaker.

Abarzuza states that on first reading, the song as transcribed has no apparent meaning although some words are recognizable. He mentions the allusion to Artajona, one of the officially recognized towns—*buenas villas*—in medieval Navarre, but he makes no real effort to sort out a story line.

José Luis Ansorena, in his book *El Euskera en la polifonía religiosa y profana*, does not attempt to translate the song, saying only that while it contains Basque it is in a strange and contradictory form. He notes—attributing the view to Barbieri—that "You Eat, We'll Eat, the Freeloaders' Ball" might be placed in the category of comedic pornographic songs.

Barbieri himself very much wanted to make the song make sense. He tells us that *jançu* is an elided form of *jan ezazu*—the command, eat! Whilte *janto dego* should be read as *jango dugu*—we'll eat! *Garcigorreta* and *garcigorrá* suggest *comer de gorraó*—*comer como capigorrones*. *Capigorrón* was a common medieval Spanish term used to pejoratively describe students at the University of Salamanca who were too poor to cover their expenses. Such students often had only a single cape—*capa*—and hat—*gorra*—and were known to attend events where there would be free food, often faking invitations or attaching themselves to someone who had been invited. So a *capigorrón* was a freeloader and *comer como capigorrones* or *comer de gorraó* meant to belly up to the table of free food.

But *gorra* was also late medieval slang for a fool, a buffoon, which leads to another supposition Barbieri made—that the song was a *vejamen*—a satiric comedic composition in which a singer points out someone else's physical and moral defects. Barbieri believed "You Eat, We'll Eat, the Freeloaders' Ball" was performed by the Emperor Carlos V's jester, who was known for his wicked biting tongue. We don't know who was being lampooned.

*Chacorra* could have been either *txakur*—dog—or *txekor*—calf. *Arre*, which exists to this day in both Spanish and Basque, has many meanings, one of which is giddy up! Get moving! This extraordinary effort on Barbieri's part goes on and on—*çei* as *zer*, the question word "what." Or maybe *çei* has some other meaning. *Gavian* as *gauean*—at night. *Vero, veroá* as *bero beroa*—hot, hot. *Estangurria* is the Basque root of the English word strangury, which is the medical term for a condition caused by blockage or irritation at the base of the bladder, resulting in severe pain and a strong desire to urinate. But maybe that has nothing to do with "You Eat, We'll Eat, the Freeloaders' Ball." Maybe it's connected more to *Eztarri*—throat.

There's a lot we don't know, including whether or not "You Eat, We'll Eat, the Freeloaders' Ball" was a *zaloma*. Pepe Rey says it's a polyphonic musical composition inspired by a *zaloma* sung by Basque sailors. In his view it's not a transcription of an actual *zaloma*. And maybe it wasn't a rowing song but a song to help hoist the sails—*gavia* can be either the crow's nest on the mainmast or the mainmast sail itself, so *gavian dani levari* could mean hoist the mainsail. As quoted by José Luis Ansorena, Pepe Rey stated his belief that "You Eat, We'll Eat, the Freeloaders' Ball" was "más como un trabalenguas que como una canción con un significado concreto" (more like a tongue twister than a song with a concrete meaning).

Leopoldo María Panero (1948-2010), while not a translator of "You Eat, We'll Eat, the Freeloaders' Ball," offered suggestive ideas for bringing the poem into English (Blesa, 2011). Panero believed translation could be used to amplify a text, to develop and go beyond the original material, to make the translation as original as the original. He called his method "translation as perversion," though the Spanish *perversión* might also be translated as wickedness, and we could indeed say Panero's practice was translation as defiance or transfiguration or enchantment. It's a method not too different from the borrowing and mixing practices of contemporary pop musicians worldwide.[42]

Finally, an interpretation of the song performed by Beltxaren Bikotea is available online.[43]

# Jançu janto dego de garcigorreta

Jançu janto, dego de garçigorreta,
jançu janto, dego de garçigorrá,
arre chacorra çei degueçu, gavian dani levari,
María Roche çerca mora en cantar viçerraco,
es naqui en Artajona por do Gurgurengoá,
por do pasa Ochoá candia jaroa por do veroá
vero vero veroá Estangurria rrico va.[44]

# You Eat, We'll Eat, the Freeloaders' Ball

You eat, we'll eat, the freeloaders' ball.
You eat, we'll eat, fool scholars all.
Heave away you dirty dogs, now at last
you'll haul that sail right up the mast.
Maria Roche, what a row.
The young bulls sing, noisy yowl.
Artajona, strange to me,
not to know the wine was free,
vintage wine, flowing fine,
hot mulled wine, finally, mine.
Hot and hotter, hot as can be,
down it goes, so easily.

# Çutegon / On My Feet

Along with "You Eat, We'll Eat, the Freeloaders' Ball," "Çutegon" is one of three songs included in Francisco Asenjo Barbieri's 1890 publication of the *Cancionero de Palacio de los siglos XV y XVI* that contain Basque words and phrases. Catalogued as number 443 in Barbieri's collection, "Çutegon," like "You Eat, We'll Eat, the Freeloaders' Ball," appears to have been transcribed by a non-Basque speaker. Words are sometimes cut in two, or part of one word is added to another. This can be seen in the first two lines of the song, printed in the Palace Songbook as "Çutegon e singuel deriquegon." The lines would be more accurately transcribed by a Basque speaker of the period as "Zut egon, ezin gueldiric egon," and by a speaker of contemporary Unified Basque—Euskara Batua—as "Zutik egon, ezin geldirik egon." Four of the seven lines in the poem—from "Por mi fé" to "es razón"—are written in standard Spanish, indicating a writer who knew that language.

While "Çutegon" can be read as a love poem, it might be a poem of love's end (looking at you each day makes me unhappy) or it might be love's impossibility (looking at you day after day, and not having you, makes me unhappy). Either way, there is a sense of unhappiness. A different reading of the song is given by Patri Urquizu in his book *Historia de la Literatura Vasca* (2000). Urquizu states that "Çutegon" is a satiric dance song. In this view, the would-be lover—anxious, nervous, and filled with longing—can't keep his feet still.

All of these readings of the poem—love coming to an end, love refused, or love yet to begin—are amplified by the switch from Basque to Spanish. Perhaps the poem's narrator—a native Spanish speaker with a weak grasp of Basque—is attempting to woo, or explain feelings to, a native Basque speaker who has a fine grasp of Spanish. The narrator starts in Basque then collapses into Spanish, hoping for the best.

# Çutegon

Çutegon
e singuel deriquegon.
Por mi fe, señora mía,
que he perdido ell alegría
en miraros cada día;
que es razón
e singuel deriquegon.[45]

# On My Feet

I'm on my feet but can't stand still.
I swear, my sweet, I was happy till
looking at you every day
I found I'd somehow lost my way,
that's the reason, it's really real—
I'm on my feet but can't stand still.[46]

# Un señora muerto habías (Juantxo Mondragonen kantua) / My Lady, You've Killed (Juantxo Mondragon's Song)

"My Lady, You've Killed" is the third of the songs Francisco Asenjo Barbieri included in his 1890 *Cancionero de Palacio* that suggest a writer with knowledge of Basque. Catalogued as number 417, the poem is one in which a male lover expresses desire for the female beloved while also reproaching her for her disdain. Feeling that she has lost interest in him, the narrator is filled with anxiety.

Unlike the two other Basque pieces in Barbieri's collection, this one is written not in Basque but in Spanish, with only three Basque words—*bai*, *fedea*, and *urdaia*—so one might think it was written by a native Spanish speaker. But there are errors of grammar and usage that imply the poem was written by a person whose first language was Basque. This is apparent in the lack of correct gender agreement between Spanish nouns, articles, and adjectives. *La calle* is here "el calle"; *una señora* is "un señora"; *señora hermosa* is "señora hermoso"; and *zapatos ricos* are "zapatos ricas." It would not be surprising for such mistakes to be made by a Basque speaker, as Basque is a language without grammatical gender. Another error appears in the author's tendency to add vowels to the beginning of words, as would be the case in Basque—"amatas" for *matas* and "errazon" for *razón*. And stressed pronouns are not always in agreement with objects—"le das a mi" rather than *me das a mi*.

To honor the complexity of language in the Basque Country where Basque, French, and Spanish sometimes take mixed forms—Frañol, Euskañol, Franskara—our translation includes *turrón*—the Spanish form of nougat thought to have come to the Iberian Peninsula from the Middle East 500 years ago—and escargot—the French delicacy made from the humble snail.

# Un señora muerto habías
# (Juantxo Mondragonen kantua)

Un señora muerto habías
a Juancho de Mondragón
y no tenías errazon.
Señora eres tan hermoso
que amatas a vida mía;
amor tuyo es tan gracioso
que le das a mi mal día.
Sabes mucha raposia,
no lo entiendo yo tu amor.
Jura a Dios, bay fedea,
que lo has mala condición.
Juro a San Miguel d'Oñate,
el que calza bragas d'oro,
si no me das a rescate,
me vevir es todo lloro.
Por el calle donde moro
le veo a missa pasar,
y en las fiestas de holgar
que amata su afición.
Darte he cosas bonicas,
muchos cuentos y manillas,
y zapatos mucho ricas,
y otras cosas maravillas;
muchos frutos y rosquillas,
nuegados y caracoles;
darte he urdaya con coles,
qu'es muy rico comezon.[47]

# My Lady, You've Killed (Juantxo Mondragon's Song)

My Lady, you've killed
Juantxo Mondragon.
It's not right. You,
who are so lovely,
have taken my life.
It's a strange love
that ruins my day.
Clever as a fox,
I don't understand.[48]

Before God and by our faith,
admit you've wronged me.
I swear by Saint Michael of Oñati,
by his garments of gold,[49]
that if you don't rescue me,
I'll spend my life in tears.

I see her pass along my street
on her way to Mass,
and at meaningless parties,
her brutal caress.

I have lovely things for you—
cunning tales, bracelets,
expensive shoes,
and other wonders—
fruits and pastries,
turrones and escargot,
bacon and cabbage,
everything good to eat.

# Nafarroako kondestablearen kanta / The Governor General of Navarre's Song

According to Francisco Aleson's 1715 Annals of the Kingdom of Navarre, this brief song was performed at the celebration in Iruñea-Pamplona following the coronation in early January 1494 of Catherine of Navarre and the Gascon nobleman Jean d'Albret III, the couple to rule as Queen Katalina and King Juan III of Navarre.

In 1483, following the death of her brother Francis Phoebus, fifteen-year-old Catherine was named queen under the regency of her mother who arranged Catherine's wedding to the then fourteen-year-old Jean d'Albret III. The marriage was to protect the kingdom from Catherine's uncle as well as from Isabel I of Castile and Fernando II of Aragon who had hoped to marry Catherine to their son Juan, Prince of Asturias. Catherine and Jean d'Albret's marriage was reportedly not consummated until 1491 when Jean—King Juan III—was twenty-two and Catherine—Queen Katalina—was twenty-three.

From 1483 to the coronation, there was increasing conflict and jockeying for political power in Navarre. At Christmas in 1493, Luis de Beaumont, Second Count of Lerin and Navarre's constable—analogous to governor general in medieval Basque and Spanish—took over Iruñea and blockaded the city. Civil war seemed imminent but following the signing of a temporary peace agreement, the January 1494 coronation took place.

Eliciting both sighs of relief and cries of regret, the coronation was followed by a week-long celebration at which songs, sometimes comedic, were performed as a way to calm nerves and tempers. One of these was "The Governor General of Navarre's Song," a call for peace between the king and queen and Beaumont. However comedic the song may have been, the count was apparently not amused, leaving before the week of celebration ended. It wasn't long before he rebelled against the new rulers. Tried and condemned for treason in 1507, he escaped and died in Aragon in 1508. His son, Luis Beaumont, third count of Lerin, also rose against the kingdom and began what was to be a ten-year-long war dividing Navarre into lands north of the Pyrenees governed by Katalina and Juan III and lands south of the Pyrenees governed by the Beaumonts who had long sought more power through betrayal. The third count's grandfather—the first count Luis—was the murderer of Bereterretxe whose story is told in an earlier poem in this book. So much for a song calming nerves and tempers.

The name Labrit mentioned in the poem refers to Jean d'Albret II and Jean d'Albret III, father and son, both known as "Labrit" in Basque.

# Nafarroako kondestablearen kanta

Labrìt, età Erreguè
aytà semè diràde,
Condestable Jauna
arbizate Anàie.[50]

# The Governor General of Navarre's Song

Labrit and the king—
father and son,
embrace the governor general
as a brother.

# Leloren kanta / Lelo's Song

"Lelo's Song" is drawn from what was said to be a five-year-long war between Basque forces led by Lelo and Lekobide and the armies of the first Roman emperor Caesar Augustus, also known as Octavian, who ruled from 27 BCE until his death in 14 CE. As with many epics, the poem's historical accuracy has been questioned. Many have held Lekobide to be a fictional character who saved the life of the equally fictional Irish exiled Prince Lemor MacMorna who became the legendary Basque hero Jaun Zuria. Notwithstanding their historical antecedents, these Irish and Basque figures are composites made from different individuals, times, and places.

The war alluded to in "Lelo's Song" may or may not have taken place in the Basque Country. The early twentieth century writer Julio Urquijo held that Caesar Augustus never entered the Basque Country, that his war in Cantabria took place to the west of what is now Bizkaia. Some say Lelo was a war leader whose wife was seduced by a man named Zara, and that Zara killed Lelo. We see this in the second line of the poem, çarac yl Leloa, where the *k* sound shown as a hard *c* at the end of çarac indicates that the word may be a proper name—Zara—used here as the subject of a transitive verb—Zarak kills Lelo. In this reading, the murder offers a truncated version of the Agamemnon story—the murder of the hero king. In most versions, though, Çarac appears as Çaray—*zara*, the second person form of the verb "to be" (you are) and there is no person named Zara, transitive or not. Accepting that, Zarak does not appear in our translation.

What about Lelo? In contemporary Basque, *lelo* has several meanings—a musical refrain, a jingle, a chant. It's also a tiring, oft repeated bit of speech, as when a person takes up a subject and won't let it go (we've heard it a million times). As to a person, *lelo* means foolish, silly, dull, dim, stupid. And in medieval poetry and song, *lelo* was used as a formulaic opening or ending to a song— lelo lelori lelori lelo—the way an English language singer might use tra-la-la-la-la. Maybe we've tried to have our cake and eat it too by opening our translation with both the formulaic musical phrase and the death of the hero Lelo.

Following Lelo's death, the poem backs up to the putative wars between the Basques and the Romans. The unknown poet reminds us that in our land or in the enemy's, the load is tied down with the same rope—tied on the cart the same way, we've said. Despite Basque victory over the numerically larger invading Roman forces, the war brought greater pain and loss to the Basques. This is revealed in the largely lost stanza that begins "Esin gueyago"—the fragmentary "Can't more." We are reminded that when you fight in your own country, your houses and crops are burned, your animals slaughtered, and your family members exiled, wounded, and killed.

In the last stanza, an unknown word appears—*uchim*. According to Julen Arriolabengoa Unzueta in his 2006 University of the Basque Country doctoral dissertation, this is Urzino, a Bizkaian military leader who took the war to Rome. After defeating the Romans, Urzino's troops were said to have settled along the Tiber River and ultimately populated much of Rome. It's possible that part of the poem has been lost and that the missing part would clarify the sudden appearance of Urzino. It's possible that Uchim is not Urzino at all, but Urtzi, also spelled Ortzi, a word associated with the sky and the ancient Basque Sky God. That offers some justification for our translation's leap to the vast expanse of sky.

"Lelo's Song" appeared in the 1558-1610 *Ibarguen-Cachopín Chronicle* (Arriolabengoa, 1996). It was first published in 1812 by Wilhelm von Humboldt in the *Königsberger* magazine. In his 1817 work *Berichtigungen und Zusätze*, von Humboldt published the same poem with extensive comments. Juan Carlos Guerra (1860-1941), who transcribed the poem from the Ibarguen materials, noted that the poem was likely written later than the fifteenth century by a highly literate Bizkaian or one who knew the Bizkaian dialect of Basque and more particularly the Basque used in the Arratia Valley. Guerra also believed that the writer was more knowledgeable in Spanish than in Basque, because he or she included a certain "primitive quality" to suggest the period and location. For more of Guerra's thoughts, see his *Los Cantares antiguos del euskera: viejos textos del idioma* (Donostia, 1924).

# Leloren kanta

Lelo yl Lelo, Lelo yl Lelo,
Leloa, çarac yl Leloa.
Otabiano munduco jauna
Lecobydi Vizcaicoa.

Romaco aronac aleguyn eta
Vizcayac daroa cansoa.
Ychasotati eta leorres
ymyny deusco molsoa.

Leor çelayac bereac dira
mendi tantayac leusoac.
Lecu yronyam gagoçanean
noc bera sendo dau gogoa.

Bost urteco egun-gabean
gueldi bagaric pochoa.
Bildurric guychi arma bardinas
oramayasu guexoa.

Sojac gogorrac badyri tuys
narru biloxa surboa.
Gureco bata il badaguyan
bost amarren galdoa.

Aec anys ta guc guichytaya
asquynyn dugu lalboa.
Gueure lurrean ta aen errian
biroch aynbaten çamoa.

Esin gueyago
[... ... ...]teta

# Lelo's Song

Lelo, lelori, lelori, lelo.
You're dead, Lelo.
Octavian rules the world
as Lekobide rules Bizkaia.

The Romans take up arms.
The Bizkaians pour out song.
On land and sea
the forces gather.

The arid plains are ours,
the high mountain caves.
Defenders well dug in,
our will is strong.

For five years we've fought,
day and night, sleepless.
With equal weapons we fear nothing,
but lacking bread—hunger hurts.

Outfitted in armor, they're snails,
while we, unencumbered, are quick.
For each of us they kill,
they lose fifty men.

But they were many and we were few.
We saw, in the end, we were through.
In their land or ours, the load
is tied on the cart the same way.

Couldn't go on,
[… … …] too much

[... ... ...]
[...]

Tiber lecua gueldico çabal
uchim tamayo grandoya.
Andi aristac gueysto sindoas
betico nayas narr doa.[51]

[... ... ...]
[...]

The wide lands along the Tiber,
the vast expanse of sky.
Even the great oak sickens
and one day will fall.

# Une mousse de Biscaye /
# A Basque Girl

A popular song during the Renaissance, "A Basque Girl" was written in French with only the last line of each stanza in Basque: "Soaz, soaz ordonarequin."

The poem tells the story of a Frenchman who meets a beautiful young Basque woman near a mill and either woos or forces himself upon her. The maiden responds to his advances with a phrase that starts plainly enough—Go, go—but ends with the ambiguous "ordonarequin." *Arekin* is the Basque ending analogous to the English preposition "with." And "ordon" is *ordua*—the hour, the time for something. Given the context, it's safe to assume she's saying, "Go away and leave me alone." An earlier English language translation had her say, "Soft, soft, all in good time." Maybe the young woman is speaking not to the young man but to herself, praying for deliverance. In our translation we settled on, "Go, go, time to go," feeling it was in keeping with a number of the possible meanings of her response, and maintained its ambiguity.

Whatever she says, it's a refusal and it's in Basque, so the young man is left in the dark. Frustrated, he points out that she is speaking neither French nor Latin and then tells her to speak a language other than Basque. Defiantly—or perhaps she doesn't understand French—she repeats the same line. It's worth mentioning the French expression *parler comme une vache espagnole*—to speak like a Spanish cow. But in the period of the poem, the expression was *parler comme une vasce espagnole*—*vasce* being the word for Basque. To speak like a Spanish Basque was to speak French badly, to be incomprehensible, to make no sense. What's important is that the young man had no idea what the young woman was saying to him. Given this, it might have been better to have left the Basque line untranslated.

While Renaissance listeners may have heard "A Basque Girl" as a love song, contemporary commentators have seen it as an example of sexual harassment. It's ironic then that there is a mass derived from the song. This mass was long attributed to the French/Flemish composer Josquin des Prez but is now listed among his works as of "doubtful" origin. Some sources consider des Prez's Flemish contemporary Heinrich Isaac to be the composer of the mass. Of the two men, Ercole I d'Este, Duke of Ferrara, said (according to the New World Encyclopedia's online entry for Josquin des Prez), "It may be true that Josquin is a better composer, . . . but Isaac is better able to get along with his colleagues." Both musicians were born around 1450 and died around 1520, so might have been familiar with "A Basque Girl," which appeared for the first time in the 1501 Venice publication of Ottaviano Petrucci's *Harmonice Musices Odhecaton*. The poem was quoted by Rabelais in *La vie de Gargantua et de Pantagruel*, the five books of which were published between 1532 and 1564. As to the mass, whoever wrote it, the score was reconstructed in 1875 by the Belgian musicologist François-Auguste Gevaert and has been performed since that time.

# Une mousse de Biscaye

Une mousse de Biscaye
L'autre jour pres une moulin
Vint a moi sans dire gaire
Moy hurtant sur mon chemin
Blanche comme un parchemin
Je la baise à mon aise
Et me dist sans faire noise:
«Soaz, soaz ordonarequin».

Je luy dis que de Biscaye
J'estoys son prochain voisin:
«Mecton nous pres ceste haie
En l'ombre soubz l'aubepin
La parlerons a butin;
Faictes tout a ma requeste»
Lors feist signe de la teste:
«Soaz, soaz ordonarequin».

...Par mon serment, vecy raige:
Ce n'est Françoys ne latin:
Parlez moy aultre langaige
Et laissez votre bisquayn.
Mectons no besongne a fin,
Parlons d'amours, je vous prie.
Lors me dist, n'en doubtez mye:
«Soaz, soaz ordonarequin».

Avoir n'en puez aultre chose,
Par ma foy, a ce matin,
Fors baiser a bouche close
Et la main sur le tetin.
...Adieu, petit musequin,

# A Basque Girl

The other day by a mill,
on my way, a Basque girl
appeared without a word,
her skin paper white.
As I would, I made to kiss
the sweet miss who said
gently, yes, could be no,
"Go, go—time to go."[53]

"I'm your neighbor," I said,
"so close to Bizkaia,"
and led her to sit in the shade
of the hawthorn by the hedge.
"Do as I say," I told her,
"we'll speak of rewards."
She, shaking her head, said,
"Go, go—time to go."

By God what is this—
neither French nor Latin.
Tell me in another tongue
and forget this Basque.
"Really," I said, "we don't
need it. Pray, speak of love."
Then she—can you believe it?—
"Go, go—time to go."

Having gotten no more
that morning, I swear,
than a kiss—mouth shut—
and a hand on her breast,
I said, "Adieu, little wench,

A Dieu soyez, ma popine.
Lors me dit la biscuayne:
«Soaz, soaz ordonarequin».[52]

tease. God be with you."
And she, Basque girl, still,
"Go, go—time to go."

# Perutxoren kanta /
# Perutxo's Song

*La Celestina* or *The Tragicomedy of Calisto and Melibea*, a late-fifteenth-century composition attributed to Fernando de Rojas, had remarkable success in Castile. Repeatedly reissued throughout the sixteenth century and translated into other languages, it was expanded by other authors such as Feliciano de Silva who published a sequel, *La Celestina, part 2* in 1534 and Gaspar Gómez de Toledo who published *La Celestina, part 3* in 1536.

The third part of the tragicomedy includes a poem in Basque that is known as "El canto de Perutxo." The poem describes Perutxo, a ruined nobleman who has a horse but no squire and so must care for the animal himself. Not one given to hard work, Perutxo dedicates himself to the pursuit of love.

Written in a burlesque tone, the poem begins with the formulaic "Lelo lirelo çarayleroba," a phonetic deformation of "Lelo yl Lelo . . . çarac yl Leloa," the phrase that begins "Leloren kanta" (Lelo's Song), another of the early Basque poems that appears in this volume. The formula also appears in "Salinasko kontea preso sartu zuteneko kanta" (The Song of Those Who Captured the Count of Salinas), and in Bernat Etxepare's 1545 poem "Sautrela." While the poem is in Basque, the brief prose introduction and postscript is entirely in Spanish—aside from the sole Basque word *oguia* (bread). Perhaps when it comes to food it's best to make sure Perutxo understands.

# Perutxoren kanta

O Perucho, Perucho que mala vida hallada le tienes: linage hidalgo, tu cauallo limpias: no falta d(e) comer un pedaço oguia, sin q(ue) trabajo tanto le tengas, juras a mi siempre cauallo a suzio mi amo le haze: y Perucho almohaçando. El nada le pena por carreras hazer en amores q(ue) tiene, entre tanto busco, otro adereçar le tengo si pide: y canta le empieço bizcuença.

Lelo lirelo çarayleroba
yaçoeguia ninçan
aurten erua
ay joat gauiraya
astor usua
lelo lirelo çarayleroba.

Ayt joat gauiraya
aztobicarra
esso amorari
gajona chala
y penas naçala
jator que dala
lelo lirelo çarayleroba.

Precioso borrico es este, que se quexa de la vida que passa y dize estar desesperado y pone se a cantar: y tal le dé Dios la salud como yo le entiendo: aunque no dexaré de responder a algunos vocablos comunes que en bizcuençe dice...[54]

# Perutxo's Song

Oh, Perutxo, what a hard life you lead! Of noble blood, you have to clean up after your horse yourself! And to put even a crust of bread on the table you have to work like a dog. That's what you say but the horse is still dirty, Master, and here's Perutxo at brunch! Nothing bothers him while he's chasing around after the loves he thinks are his. Meanwhile I'm trying to track him down. I have songs of my own to sing—if he asks for one, I'll sing it to him in Basque.

Lelo lirelo zaraileroba.
Last year I was sick,
this year I'm out of my head—
the sparrow hawk has flown,
the goshawk and the pigeon,
Lelo lirelo zaraileroba.

The sparrow hawk is gone.
Donkey's beard!
Tell my lover
that I'm sick,
that I'm suffering,
that I'm on my way.
Lelo lirelo zaraileroba.

This fool of a donkey's a real charmer—complaining about the life he leads, claiming he's desperate, breaking into song. May God give him good health insofar as that's possible, and I'll never refuse to respond to the simple Basque words he uses.

# Alostorrea /
# The Alos Tower

This late medieval ballad is reminiscent of both the French fairy tale *Cinderella* in its depiction of a cruel stepmother and of the Greek epic poem *The Odyssey* in its depiction of the long-absent hero returning home to a scene of deceit. One version of the story goes like this:

Once upon a time there was a nobleman of Deba, Lord of the Alos Tower, named Beltran Perez Aloskoa, whose wife gave him a daughter the couple named Usua. Usua was as beautiful as her mother and as kind and good, but, as often happens, the child's mother died, and her widowed father remarried. While father and daughter loved each other deeply, Usua's stepmother felt no love for her husband's child. A clever woman, the stepmother never revealed her true feelings in the presence of her husband.

But Beltran Perez was an observant man and could see how his daughter suffered. Preparing to take part in the Christian wars to expel the last Muslim rulers from the Iberian Peninsula, the concerned father arranged for his daughter's marriage, hoping this would protect Usua from her stepmother's cruelty. Following the nuptial celebrations, Beltran Perez left and was gone for seven years.

In that seventh year, Usua's stepmother wrote to her husband telling him that his beloved daughter had given birth to an illegitimate child, a bastard son, and that mother and son brought shame to the family name. Heartbroken, Beltran Perez returned, but when he came in sight of the tower, rather than going directly home, he rode to a nearby inn. There, wondering what to do, he overheard two men talking loudly as they had dinner.

"I understand the master's come back."

"Yes, I've heard that, too. Imagine the surprise he'll get—leaving two at home and returning to find three."

Beltran Perez had no wish to hear any more but as the two men got up to go to their rooms, they continued their conversation.

"They say it's Usua's child."

"They can say what they like, but to my eye the kid looks a lot more like the lady of the house."

This stopped Beltran Perez in his tracks. Whatever it might take, he would find the truth. He spoke with some of his faithful servants, asking them to spread the news that he'd been killed in battle and then to put both him and his sword in a casket and take it to the Alos Tower.

The news of the death of Beltran Perez quickly spread and soon the house was filled with family, friends, and neighbors lamenting the loss of such a noble gentleman. Observing the custom of the *gaubela*—the wake—the mourners sat up all night with the body. One by one, they approached the open casket to offer their farewell and last words to the deceased.

When Usua's turn came, she leaned over and kissed her dead father on the forehead. Then she spoke, telling him she'd not set foot in the Alos Tower for the seven years he'd been gone. She alluded to what had happened in his absence, mentioning the windowless tower, the long flight of stairs to the top, and, most importantly, the black crow—*bela beltza*—cawing, cawing at the window.

Ah, but there are no windows in the Alos Tower. Where is the crow? How did he get in? Everyone knows Bela Beltza is the nickname of a young man, the illegitimate son of one of Beltran Perez's cousins. Some people are beginning to squirm. As Usua goes on, it grows ever more obvious who the new child's mother is. And who the father. Drawing his sword, the Black Crow rises from his seat on the bench by the casket. When he moves to kill Usua, Beltran Perez rises, too—clever man to have faked his own death—and taking the sword that lies with him, drives the blade side to side through Bela Beltza.

Never again would the voice of the crow be heard in the Alos Tower.

The story has long been popular along the Basque coast from Deba to Leikeitio, partly because the Alos Tower's ruins stood in Deba, Gipuzkoa, until 1844 as a dark reminder of intrigue and deceit—the affair between the stepmother and the young man who is the son of Beltran Perez's cousin; the letter from the stepmother falsely accusing Usua of adultery and of giving birth to an illegitimate son; Beltran Perez's faked death and his murder of his wife's lover. While Usua tells us that she's not set foot in the tower during the seven years of her father's absence, there remains the possibility that she knew of her stepmother's affair and chose not to reveal this to her father while he was away at war. Maybe to protect him? She does offer a character reference for herself, noting that she accepted her father's choice of husband and that she observed the customary three days of chastity following her marriage.

For another version of this story, in Basque and Spanish and including illustrations, see the City of Deba, Gipuzkoa's website.[55]

While there is uncertainty about the date of composition for "The Alos Tower," we know that Beltran Perez was away fighting Muslim forces, which places the story within the time frame of the Reconquista—the nearly eight hundred years in which Christian armies fought to end Muslim rule on the Iberian Peninsula and which ended with the fall of Granada in January, 1492. If "Alostorrea" was written in the time it was set, its latest date of composition would be near the end of the fifteenth century. The ballad was passed down orally until 1866 when it was printed in Juan V. Araquistain's *Tradiciones Vasco-Cantabras* (Basque-Cantabrian Traditions).

## Alostorrea

Etxe eder leyo bage onetan
ez naiz sartu zaspi urte aubetan;
eta zortzigarrenian,
neretzat zorigaitzian,
aita Beltran'en iltzian.

Ama-andria neria nizaz
bi erdi egin zanian,
mila olo il eta
ezkaratzian,
zazpi zezen korritu ere
enparantzian.
Ni ere banenguen
lumatxo artian,
eta nire ama-andria
urre gortiña artian.

Gero Bidania gustian
bat zan erorik eta zororik.
Aita-jauna neriak aura
senartzat eman dit;
baña ez nuke trukatuko
obiagoagatik.

Aita-jauna neriak
niri eman zidan
imiñan dotia;
ama-andriak ere ixillik
bere partia.

# The Alos Tower

Seven years I've not set foot
in this house—beautiful,
windowless. In the eighth,
misfortune draws me back—
the death of my father.

When my noble mother
brought me into this world,
they killed a thousand chickens
in the scullery
and ran seven bulls
in the plaza
while I lay
on a downy bed,
her grace, my mother
behind a curtain of gold.

Later, in all Bidania
there was one mad
fool—the man my noble
father gave me as husband,
the man I wouldn't
trade for any other.

My father gave me
a fine dowry, too,
my gracious mother
quietly adding
her part.

Lenen gabian
begiak biotzak luen mendian.
Baita berriz ere bigarrenian.
Irugarrena igaro baño len
ondo poztu zinon Alos-torria
eldu zalako neregan semia.

Alos-torria! Bai Alos-torria!
Alos-torreko eskaiera luzia
Alos-torria nenguanian
goruetan
bela beltzak kua kua
leyuetan.
Andik jaiki eta
urre goruaz jo nuan,
berri gaiztuak jo ninduan.

Zaldunak esan zion: ixil, ixil!
Ama, dolorkumia,
ez zela ori zure
esateria.

Ixil, ixil zaldun odol!
txareko gastia.
Ala ere gutxiago zan
zure eginpidia!

Aizpa edarrak or daude,
ederrik eta galantik,
atz ederrak erastunez
beterik,
ez daukatela mantubetan
zolorik;

On the first night, eyes
closed, my heart slept.
And on the second. Before
the third had passed, happiness
filled the Alos Tower,
the son I carried within.

Alos Tower, oh Alos Tower!
The long staircase
to the top where I sat
spinning, the black crow
caw, caw, cawing
at the window.
I rose and struck him
with the golden spindle
while he struck me with gossip.

Be still, the noble gentleman
ordered. Oh, Mother, this
despicable daughter,
it's not for her to speak.

It's you who should
be still, ignoble callous
young man. Even less
is it yours to speak.

There are my beautiful sisters—
all grace and elegance,
their lovely fingers
glittering with rings,
not a tear in their
cloaks,

ala ere gutxiago
begietan negarrik.

Ama-andriari ere bai
poza dario,
nere biotzari bakarrik
mindura jariyo.

Àita-jauna neria
Gaztelan zanian,
ixil askorik jayo zan
Alos-torrian semia;
eta ala ere ixilagorik
dago bakian
azitzen Zarauz aldian,
gure jatorriaren loitukerian.

Ai! Au mindura beltza,
ai! nere lotsa!
Alabak negarra ta
aitak lur otza!
Zeñek loitu zaitu zu,
Alos-torria?
Ai, ene aita maite.
Aita matia!
iltzia ondo egin duzu
aita-jaun maitia!

not a tear in their
eyes.

For my lady mother,
contentment and joy.
For my heart,
bitterness and pain.

While my noble father
was gone in Castile,
in the Alos Tower a wall
of silence hid the birth
of a son now being raised
in Zarautz, in peace.
Silence greater still,
disgrace our name.

Oh, such dark misery!
The shame I feel!
For the daughter, tears.
For the father, cold earth.
Who has dishonored
you, Alos Tower?
Oh, my dear Father,
respected Father,
you did well to die,
noble beloved Father.

# Testamentuaren balada / Last Words

In his 1953 *Romancero Hispánico*, Ramón Menéndez Pidal wrote that this ballad derives from the Castilian romance "La muerte del Príncipe Juan," composed to commemorate the 1497 death of Prince Juan, the son of Isabel of Castile and Fernando of Aragon.

Passed down orally for centuries, there are now more than a hundred versions of this song in Spanish, Portuguese, and Basque. Believed to have originally been presented as a conversation between a dying man and his lover, the poem now appears as a monologue told by a dying man to the lover lying at his side. This and other changes over time make it difficult to assess the historical accuracy of the story. And in the Basque version, the difficulty is greater as the dying man is nameless. No details about him or his life are given. Maybe he's Prince Juan but maybe not. Nor are we given any clues as to the identity of the lover who listens in silence as the dying man dictates not so much a last will and testament as a romantic and passionately religious, if unorthodox, farewell, reminding his lover and the reader of the importance of fulfilling the last wishes of those facing imminent death.

While the lover's identity remains hidden, we do learn that she is not the dying man's wife but his mistress—he tells her to sing with the choir at the funeral, something a wife would not do. We also get a glimmer of the dying man's personality when the doctors tell him he's dying of lovesickness and he responds, "It's not lovesickness killing me though I admit I'm lovesick." Whether it's a sardonic response, or he's simply sorrowful, is up to interpretation. As an unmarried couple, the lovers couldn't be together in life, and now death will separate them forever unless, as the dying man hopes, all will rejoice in the glory of Heaven where they will see each other again. This of course ignores the problem of wife and lover both showing up in Heaven.

Accepted as being a work from the late fifteenth century, "Testamentuaren balada" was collected by Resurreccion M. Azkue in three different versions and published as "Izar Ederak" (I, II, III, numbers 849, 850, 851) in his 1919 work *Cancionero popular vasco*.

## Testamentuaren balada

Izar ederrak argi egiten dau zeru altuan bakarrik;
ezta bakarrik, lagunak ditu Jaun Zerukoak emonik.
Zazpi aingeru aldean ditu, zortzigarrena gaixorik;
zazpi mediku ekarri deutsez India-Madriletatik.
Arek igarri, arek igarri nundik dagoan gaixorik:
—Amore-minak badituz onek desentraiñetan sarturik.
—Guzurra diño mediku onek. Nik eztot amore-miñik.
Amore-miñak badaukadaz be desentrainetan sarturik.
Gaur arratsean ilgo naz eta etorri gorpu-ondora,
errosario zuri eder bat esku artean dozula.
Neu enterretan naroenean igongo dozu korura,
andixek bera salto egingo'zu Birjina Amaren ortura.
Larrosea ta krabeliñea artungo dozuz eskura,
jente guztiak esan daiela neure lutua dozula.
Aingerutxoak esaten dabe Salbean Abe Maria,
gero guztiok gozatu daigun zeru altuan gloria.
Amen Abe Maria.

# Last Words

A single beautiful star lighting the sky.
Alone, not lonely, companions given
by the Lord above—seven angels beside
an eighth, fallen ill. From the Indies
and Madrid, seven doctors hum and think.
The diagnosis—half guess—it's lovesickness
killing you. Untrue! It's not lovesickness
killing me though I admit I'm lovesick.

I'll die this afternoon and you'll lie beside me,
in your hands a lovely white rosary. As they
lower me into the earth, you'll rise with the choir,
rise again to the Virgin Mary's burial ground,
in your hands the rose and the carnation.
The people will see and say it is for me
you mourn, the cherubim will recite
the Hail Mary, that we be saved to rejoice
in the glory of Heaven. Hail Mary, amen.

# Atarratzeko jauregian /
# In the Atarratze Palace

While the Zuberoan writer and cultural activist Jean-Louis Davant holds that "Atarratzeko jauregian" was written around 1585, other historians and scholars believe the ballad is from an earlier time. Whatever the original composition date, the poem is included here as it reflects the sensibility of the Basque medieval lyric and because it is one of the last examples of anonymous Basque epic poetry.[56]

Another opinion is that of nineteenth-century historian and literary critic Jean Jaurgain who tells us that the narrative chronicles the 1587 marriage of his ancestor Maria Jaurgain of the House of Ozaze in Atarratze, Zuberoa, to Charles de Luxe, a leader of the 1567-70 Catholic insurgency against Queen Joana d'Albret who sought to make Navarre a Protestant kingdom. Following the defeat of the Catholic forces, Charles crossed the Pyrenees to southern Navarre and exile in Otsagi, returning to Zuberoa after Queen Joana's death in 1572. If indeed the marriage took place in 1587, Charles was fifty-two years old and Maria was seventeen.

Another view of the ballad is given by Jesús Antonio Cid of the Complutense University's Menéndez Pidal Institute. Listing a dozen known versions of the ballad, Cid states that it relates neither to the presumed historical fact of the marriage of Charles and Maria nor to the couple's ensuing exile as a result of the Catholic Protestant conflict in the north of Navarre. Cid, along with other scholars, including the linguistic historian and Basque translator Jean-Baptiste Orpustan, believes that the Atarratze ballad combines many medieval stories and legends that feature a young woman forced against her will to marry a wealthy older man. In such stories, conflict commonly arises over where the couple is to live—in the bride's homeland or the groom's—with a common resolution of the problem being the death of the wife, often by suicide.

A contemporary version of the story appears in the song "Amak ezkondu ninduen," in which a fifteen-year-old girl begs her mother not to force her to marry a man of eighty. Unconvinced by her mother's argument that the old man will die soon and leave her financially well-off and, consequently, free, the girl says she'd rather jump out the window.[57]

With the passage of time, bits and piece of the various versions of the ballad have leaked into one another. These include the king of Hungary as a replacement for Charles as the groom, and the unannounced intrusion of Klara—Saint Clara—as the bride. Jesús Antonio Cid comments on other admixtures, including the word *Sala* which originally indicated the home of the groom and later the groom himself, and the presence of the house of Ozaze, an element Cid claims was added by Jean Jaurgain.

Nineteenth-century transcriptions of the ballad can be found in *Chants populaires de la Navarre et des Provinces Basques* (1855) by Agosti Xaho; *Le Pays Basque: sa population, sa langue, ses moeurs, sa littérature et sa musique* (1857) by Francisque-Xavier Michel; *Chants populaires du Pays Basque* (1870) by Jean D. J. Sallaberri; and *Quelques légendes poétiques du Pays de Soule* (1899) by Jean de Jaurgain. The version presented here is Jaurgain's as it appears in *Euskal kantutegia* (The Basque Songbook) from the Society for Basque Studies. Antonio Zavala included many versions of the song in his 1998 book *Euskal erromantzeak*.[58] Of those versions, Jaurgain's is the only one that opens with the line, "Ozaze Jaurgainean bi zitru doratü." The others all begin with some form of the line "Atharratze jauregian bi zitroiñ doratü" (Two golden lemons at the Atarratze Palace).

# Atarratzeko jauregian

Ozaze Jaurgainean bi zitru doratü
Atharratzeko jaunak bata dü galtatü
üken dü arrapostü ez direla hontü
hontürik direnean batto ükenen dü.

Atharratzeko hiria, hiri ordoki
hur handi bat badizü alde bateti(k)
errege bidea erdi erditi(k)
Maria Maidalena beste aldeti(k).

—Portaleala joan zite ahizpa maitea
engoitik horra düzü Atharratzeko jauna
—otoi erranizozü ni eri nizala
zazpi egün hoietan ohean nizala.

—Bai bena ez nükezü hortan sinetsia
hari erraiten bad(ei)ot zü eri zirela,
zazpi egün hoietan ohean zirela
bera nahi dükezü jin zü ziren leküala.

—Ahizpa jauntsezazü arropa xuria
nik ere jauntsiren dit ene zaia berdea;
engoiti horra düzü zure senargeia
botzik kita ezazü zure sortetxea.

—Klara zoaza orai salako leihora
iparra ala hegoa denez jakitera
iparra balinbada goraintzi Salari
ene korpitzaren txerka(ra) jin dadila sarri.

—Ama joanen gira oro alkarreki
etxerat jinen zira xangri handireki

# In the Atarratze Palace

At Jaurgain's in Ozaze are two golden lemons.
The Lord of Atarratze asks for one
and is told they aren't ripe.
When they are, one will be his.

Atarratze—city on the prairie,
on one side a wide river,
on the other Mary Magdalene's Way,
the King's Road through the center.

Go to the gate, Sister dear,
where the Lord of Atarratze waits.
Tell him, please, I'm sick,
I've lain in bed for a week.

Fine, but I wouldn't believe that.
And if I tell him you're sick,
that you've lain in bed a week,
he'll want to come inside.

Put on your white gown, Sister.
I'll wear my green skirt.
Your husband-to-be is here.
Be glad as you leave home.

Go to the palace window, Klara,
to see what comes north or south.
If north, remember me to Sala,
that he come for my corpse.

All of us, Mother, will go.
You'll return in sorrow,

bihotza kargatürik, begiak bustirik
eta zure alaba tonban ehortzirik.

—Ama saldü naizü biga bat bezala
bai eta desterratü oi Espainialat
aita bizi üken banü ama zü bezala
ez nündüzün ezkontüren Atharratze Salala.

Ozazeko zeinüak dü arrapikatzen
jaurgainek(o) anderea herritik partitzen
haren peko zaldia ürrez da zelatzen
hanko ttipi-handiak beltzez dira beztitzen.[59]

heart heavy, weeping,
your daughter in her grave.

Mother, you sold me like a calf,
shipped me to Spain, married me off
to Sala of Atarratze. If Father were
alive, he'd never have done this.

The bells are ringing in Atarratze,
the Lady of Jaurgain leaving home,
her faithful mare saddled in gold,
young and old dressed in black.

# Atarratzeko jauregian (bigarren bertsioa) / In the Atarratze Palace (second version)

This is the version of "Atarratzeko jauregian" that appears in Jean D. J. Sallaberri's 1870 publication *Chants populaires du Pays Basque*. While this and the preceding version present a similar narrative and theme, Sallaberri's ballad differs from Jaurgain's in several ways. Some changes are orthographic, reflecting the absence of standardized spelling for Basque until quite recently. More substantial changes are seen in the story itself. In Sallaberri, the young woman's forced marriage is not to the Lord of Atarratze but to the King of Hungary. As Sallaberri tells it, the bride-to-be is in love with Atarratze. She has chosen a husband and her choice is being denied. Another change in Sallaberri's version is that the parent arranging the forced marriage is no longer the mother, but now the widowed father making the sale. Finally, in Sallaberri, the singer expresses more strongly the depth of the bride-to-be's resistance to the marriage. When she asks her sister to tell the waiting king of Hungary that she is ill, she says she has lain in bed not for a week—seven days—but for seven years. As she was said to be seventeen at the time of the marriage, that would make her no older than ten when she fell ill and took to her bed.

In 1611, arranged marriages such as those described in the ballad were declared illegal in the Kingdom of Navarre. Parents and grandparents were from that time forward forbidden to force their children and grandchildren to marry against their will.

# Atarratzeko jauregian
# (bigarren bertsioa)

Atharratze jauregian bi zitroiñ doratü;
ongriako erregek batto dü galthatü;
arrapostü ükhen dü eztirela huntü,
huntü direnian batto ükhenen dü.

Atharratzeko hiria hiri ordoki,
hur handi bat badizü alde bateti;
errege bidia erdi erditi,
Maria-Maidalena beste aldeti.

—Aita, saldü naizü idi bat bezala;
ama bizi ükhen banü, aita, zü bezala,
enündüzün ez juanen Ongrian behera,
bena bai ezkuntüren Atharratzeko Salala.

—Ahizpa, juan zite portaliala,
ingoiti horra düzü Ongriako erregia;
—hari erran izozü ni eri nizala,
zazpi urthe huntan ohian nizala.

—Ahizpa, enükezü ez sinhetsia,
zazpi urthe huntan ohian zirela;
zazpi urthe huntan ohian zirela;
bera nahi dükezü jin zü zien lekhila.

—Ahizpa jaunts ezazü arrauba berdia,
ni ere jauntsiren dit ene churia;
ingoiti horra düzü Ongriako erregia;
botzik kita ezazü zure sor etchia.

# In the Atarratze Palace (second version)

Two golden lemons at the Atarratze Palace.
The King of Hungary asks for one
and is told they aren't ripe.
When they are, one will be his.

Atarratze—city on the prairie,
on one side a wide river,
on the other Mary Magdalene's Way,
the King's Road through the center.

Father, you've sold me like an ox.
If Mother were alive, she wouldn't
ship me off to Hungary as you will.
I'd marry the Lord of Atarratze.

Go to the gate, Sister,
where the King of Hungary waits.
Tell him, please, I'm sick,
I've lain in bed for seven years.

Sister, he won't believe that,
that you've lain in bed for seven years,
that you've lain in bed for seven years.
He'll want to come inside.

Put on your green gown, Sister.
I'll wear my white one.
The King of Hungary is here.
Be glad as you leave home.

—Aita, zü izan zira ene saltzale,
anaie gehiena dihariren hartzale,
anaie artekua zamariz igaraile,
anaie chipiena ene lagüntzale.

—Aita, juanen gira oro alkharreki;
etcherat jinen zira changri handireki,
bihotza kargatürik, begiak bustirik,
eta zure alhaba thumban ehortzirik.

—Ahizpa, zuza orai Salako leihora,
ipharra ala hegua denez jakitera;
ipharra balimbada goraintzi Salari
ene khorpitzaren cherka jin dadila sarri.

Atharratzeko zeñiak berak arrapikatzen;
hanko jente gazteriak beltzez beztitzen,
andere Santa-Klara hantik phartizten;
haren peko zamaria ürhez da zelatzen.[60]

Father, a salesman trading my flesh.
Older brother taking the money.
Middle brother lifting me onto the mare.
Younger brother who would help me.

All of us, Father, will go.
You'll return in sorrow,
heart heavy, weeping,
your daughter in her grave.

Go to the palace window, Sister,
to see what comes north or south.
If north, remember me to Sala,
that he come for my corpse.

The bells are ringing in Atarratze,
the young people dressed in black,
the Lady Saint Clara leaving,
her faithful mare saddled in gold.

# Bibliography

Aleson, Francisco de, *Tomo quinto de los Annales de Navarra ò segundo de su segunda parte*, Iruñea-Pamplona, [s.e.], 1715.

Ansorena, José Luis, "El euskera en la polifonía religiosa y profana," Piarres Laffiteri omenaldia, 1983, pp. 107-125.

Ansorena, José Luis, "La música en el mar. Itsas Memoria," *Revista de Estudios Marítimos del País Vasco*, No. 6, 2009, pp. 459-478.

Aralar, José, *La victoria de Munguía y la reconciliación de oñazinos y ganboinos*, Ekin, Buenos Aires, 1949.

Arriolabengoa, Julen, "Erdi Aroko kanta ezezagunak Ibarguen-Cachopin kronikan (1570-1620). Butroeko Andrearen Eresiaren bertsio ezezaguna; Salinasko Kontearen Kantua; Errodrigo Zaratekoaren Kantu Epikoa," *Anuario del Seminario de Filología Vasca "Julio de Urquijo,"* 30-31, 1996, pp. 71-98.

Barbieri, Francisco A., *Cancionero de Palacio de los siglos XV y XVI transcrito y comentado por Francisco Asenjo Barbieri*, Real Academia de Bellas Artes de San Fernando, Madrid, 1890.

Billelabeitia, Miren; Kortazar, Jon (Eds.), *Euskal baladak eta kantu herrikoiak = Baladas y canciones tradicionales vascas*, Centro de Lingüística Aplicada Atenea, Madrid, 2011.

Blesa, Túa, "Teoría y práctica de la traducción como perversión." In Panero, Leopoldo María, *Traducciones / Perversiones*. Madrid, Visor Libros, 2011.

Carlos, Abelardo de (Ed.), *La Ilustración española y americana*, Gaspar y Roig, Madrid, 1897.

Cid, Jesús Antonio. "Re-deconstruyendo la balada: «Atharratze jauregian»." *Anuario del Seminario de Filología Vasca Julio de Urquijo* 44, no. 2 (2010): 155-220.

Davant, Jean-Louis, *Zuberoako literaturaz. Antologia laburra*, Euskaltzaindia, Bilbo, 2008.

Davant, Jean-Louis, *Ozaze Jaurgainean. Jean de Jaurgainen Züberoa Herriko kondaira poetiko zonbait*, Euskaltzaindia, Bilbo, 2020.

Dechepare, Bernat, *Linguae Vasconum primitiae* = *The first fruits of the Basque language*, Center for Basque Studies Press, Reno, Nevada, 2012.

Fernandez de Larrea, Jon Andoni, "Lucha de bandos y guerra a sangre y fuego," *Anuario del Seminario de Filología Vasca "Julio de Urquijo,"* pp. 697-698.

Gevaert, Auguste (Ed.), *Chansons du XVe Siècle: Publiées d'après le manuscrit de la Bibliothèque Nationale de Paris par Gaston Paris et accompagnées de la musique transcrite en notation moderne par Auguste Gevaert*, Didot, Paris, 1875.

García Salazar, Lope de, *Istoria de las bienandanças e fortunas*, [s.l.], 1476.

Garibay, Esteban de, *Compendio historial de las Chronicas y Universal Historia de todos los Reynos d'España*, Christophoro Plantino, Antwerpen, 1571.

Griffin, Alan, *La puerta abierta: baladas vascas e internacionales*, Aztarna, Hernani, 2023.

Guerra, Juan Carlos de (Ed.), *Los Cantares antiguos del euskera: viejos textos del idioma*, Martín y Mena, Donostia, 1924.

Irujo, Xabier; Álvarez, Amaia (Eds.), *The Basque Medieval City: The Laws of Estella and San Sebastian in the Twelfth Century*, Center for Basque Studies Press, University of Nevada, Reno 2019.

Isasti, Lope de, *Compendio historial de la provincia de Guipuzcoa, por Lope de Isasti en el año de 1625*, Ignacio Ramon Baroja, Donostia, 1850.

Jaurgain, Jean de, *Quelques légendes poétiques du pays de Soule*, 1899.

Jaurgain, Jean de, "Quelques légendes poétiques du pays de Soule," In *La Tradition au Pays Basque. Ethnographie, folklore, art populaire, histoire, hagiographie*, Bureaux de la Tradition Nationale, Paris, 1899.

Kaltzakorta, Jabier (Ed.), *Euskal baladak: azterketa eta edizio kritikoa* = Basque Ballads: Analysis and Critical Edition, Editores Muelle de Uribitarte, Bilbao, 2017.

Leizaola, Jesús M., *El Refranero vasco antiguo y la poesia euskerica*, Ekin, Buenos Aires, 1978.

*Memorial histórico español: Colección de documentos, opúsculos y antigüedades que publica la Real Academia de la Historia*, Imprenta de José Rodríguez, Madrid, 1834.

Mendieta, Francisco de, *Quarta parte de los Annales de Vizcaya que Francisco de Mendieta, vecino de Vilbao, recopiló por mandado del señorío*, Hijos de J. Baroja, Donostia, 1915.

Menéndez Pelayo, Marcelino, *Obras Completas: Orígenes de la novela*, Universidad de Cantabria, Santander, 2018.

Menéndez Pidal, Ramón, *Romancero hispánico*, Espasa-Calpe, Madrid, 1953.

Menéndez y Pelayo, Marcelino, *Antología de poetas líricos castellanos: desde la formación del idioma hasta nuestros días*, Librería Hernando, Madrid, 1900.

Michel, Francisque, *Le Pays Basque: sa population, sa langue, ses moeurs, sa littérature et sa musique*, Firmin Didot frères, fils et Cie, 1857.

Mitxelena, Koldo, *Textos arcaicos vascos*, Minotauro, Madrid, 1964.

Moguel, Juan Antonio, *El doctor Peru Abarca ... ó Diálogos entre un rústico solitario bascongado y un barbero callejero llamado maisu Juan*, J. de Elizalde, Durango, 1881.

Muxika, Luis M., *Historia de la literatura euskerika*, L. Haranburu, Donostia, 1979.

Orpustan, Jean-Baptiste. *Précis d'histoire littéraire basque, 1545-1950: cinq siècles de littérature en euskara*. Izpegi, 1996.

Otazu, Alfonso, "El Cantar de Bretaña. Un poema inédito de fines del siglo XV en la lengua vasca," *Anuario del Seminario de Filología Vasca "Julio de Urquijo,"* vol. 7, No.19, 1975, pp. 43-70.

Paden, William D., *The Medieval Pastourelle*, Garland Pub., New York, 1987.

Paya, Xabier, *Ahozko euskal literaturaren antologia = Antología de literatura oral vasca = Anthology of Basque oral literature*, Etxepare Euskal Institutua, Donostia, 2013.

Peillen, Txomin, "Altzürükü Urrutiako leinuaren eresiak XV. mendeko," *Euskera*, XXXI (2.aldia), 1986, pp. 75-77.

Rabelais, François, *Les oevvres de M. François Rabelais ... contenant cinq liures de la vie ... de Gargantua et son filz Pantagruel*, Pour Pierre Estiard, Lyon, 1574.

Rey, Pepe, "Jançu janto, una zaloma," *Musiker*, No. 13, 2002, pp. 59-65.

Saenz Abarzuza, Igor, "Jançu Janto y el acto creativo de la traducción paneresca como per-versión," *Sonograma: Revista de pensament musical i difusió cultural en V.O., ISSN 1989-1938*. No. 044, October 29, 2019. https://sonograma.org/2019/10/jancu-janto-y-el-acto-creativo-de-la-traduccion/

Sallaberri, Jean Dominique Julien. *Chants populaires du Pays Basque. Paroles et musique originales, recueillies et publiées avec traduction française par JDJ Sallaberry.* Basq. and Fr. 1870.

Urkizu, Patricio, "Viejas baladas vascas del cancionero de Chaho," *Revista de lenguas y literaturas catalana, gallega y vasca*, No. 11, 2005, pp. 65-66.

Urquizu, Patri, *Historia de la Literatura Vasca*, UNED, Madrid, 2000.

Velasco y Fernández de la Cuesta, Ladislao de, *Los Euskaros en Álava, Guipúzcoa y Vizcaya: sus orígenes, historia, lengua, leyes, costumbres y tradiciones*, Imp. de Oliveres a Cargo de A. Xumetra, Barcelona, 1879.

Yztueta, Juan Ygnacio de, *Guipuzcoaco Provinciaren Condaira edo Historia*, Ignacio Ramon Baroja, Donostia, 1847.

Zaldibia, Juan Martínez de, *Historia guipuzcoana*, manuscript, Tolosa, [ca. 1560].

Zavala, Antonio, *Euskal erromantzeak*, Sendoa Argitaletxea, Oiartzun, Gipuzkoa, 1998.

# Notes

1   Garibay, Esteban de, *Compendio historial de las Chronicas y Universal Historia de todos los Reynos d'España*, Christophoro Plantino, Antwerpen, 1571, lib. 26, p. 300. And Mitxelena, Koldo, *Textos arcaicos vascos*, Minotauro, Madrid, 1964, p. 66.

2   Zaldibia, Juan Martínez de, *Historia guipuzcoana*, manuscript, Tolosa, [ca. 1560].

3   Zaldibia, Juan Martínez de, *Historia guipuzcoana*, manuscript, Tolosa, [ca. 1560]. This is also found, with some changes, in Garibay, Esteban de, *Compendio historial de las Chronicas y Universal Historia de todos los Reynos d'España*, Christophoro Plantino, Antwerpen, 1571, lib. 26, p. 300. And Mitxelena, Koldo, *Textos arcaicos vascos*, Minotauro, Madrid, 1964, p. 66.

4   Mitxelena, Koldo, *Textos arcaicos vascos*, Minotauro, Madrid, 1964, pp. 69-73.

5   Guerra, Juan Carlos de (Ed.), *Los Cantares antiguos del euskera: viejos textos del idioma*, Martín y Mena, Donostia, 1924, pp. 7-10. http://www.liburuklik.euskadi.eus/jspui/handle/10771/24407

6   Urruxolako kanta (1400-1588). Klasikoen Gordailua: https://klasikoak.armiarma.eus/testuak/herri14004.htm
There is a second version by the Basque linguist Koldo Mitxelena:
Gaiça çenduan leinztarroc Urruxolako lecayoa,
Sendo çenduan odolori biurtu jaçu gaçatua.

7   "Título de cómo pelearon en Unçueta los Ganboanos e los Butrón e cómo fueron vençidos los Ganboanos e muerto Juan de Ibargoen e otros muchos." García Salazar, Lope de, *Istoria de las bienandanças e fortunas*, 1476, lib. 22, fol. 399.

8   Mitxelena, Koldo, *Textos arcaicos vascos*, Minotauro, Madrid, 1964, p. 69. See the edition by Ana María Marín

at: http://parnaseo.uv.es/Lemir/Textos/bienandanzas/Menu.htm. See also: Aramburu, Enrique Jorge, *La lengua más antigua de Europa: el vasco en su literatura y apellidos*, Editorial Biblos, 2001, p. 44.

9  Peillen, Txomin, "Altzürükü Urrutiako leinuaren eresiak XV. mendeko," *Euskera*, XXXI (2.aldia), 1986, pp. 69-85. https://www.euskaltzaindia.eus/dok/euskera/euskera_1986_1.pdf

10 To read this contemporary take on the ancient theme, see: Peillen, Txomin, "Altzürükü Urrutiako leinuaren eresiak XV. mendeko," *Euskera*, XXXI (2.aldia), 1986, pp. 75-77. See also, Jean de Jaurgain, "Quelques légendes poétiques du Pays de Soule," in *La Tradition du Pays Basque*, Bureaux de la Tradition Nationale, Paris, 1899, pp. 361-365.

For a complete version visit: http://basquepoetry.eus/?i=poemak&b=1

11 Griffin, Alan, *La puerta abierta*, Aztarna, Hernani, 2023, pp. 234-239.

12 Urkizu, Patricio, "Viejas baladas vascas del cancionero de Chaho," *Revista de lenguas y literaturas catalana, gallega y vasca*, No. 11, 2005, pp. 65-66. And, Leizaola, Jesús M., *El Refranero vasco antiguo y la poesía euskerica*, Ekin, Buenos Aires, 1978.

13 http://basquepoetry.eus/?i=poemak&b=27. See, Jean de Jaurgain, "Quelques légendes poétiques du Pays de Soule," in *La Tradition du Pays Basque*, Bureaux de la Tradition Nationale, Paris, 1899, pp. 368-371.

14 This and the preceding stanza were introduced in Pierre Lafitte's 1967 version of the poem. According to Jean-Louis Davant, they were added in Pier Paul Berzaitz's pastoral. Davant, Jean-Louis, *Zuberoako literaturaz. Antologia laburra*, Euskaltzaindia, Bilbo, 2008, p. 5.

15 Mitxelena, Koldo, *Textos arcaicos vascos*, Minotauro, Madrid, 1964, pp. 79-80.

16 "Título de cómo los de Gelapa e Ganboínos e de Avendaño mataron a Gómez González e otros muchos e de la causa d'ello e cómo morió el dicho Gómez González." García Salazar, Lope de, *Istoria de las bienandanças e fortunas*, 1476, lib. 22, fol. 399.

17 http://basquepoetry.eus/?i=poemak&b=825

18 The original source document uses Joaniko and the earlier named Joanikote to identify a single person.

19 Arriolabengoa, Julen, "Erdi Aroko kanta ezezagunak Ibarguen-Cachopin kronikan (1570-1620). Butroeko Andrearen Eresiaren bertsio ezezaguna; Salinasko Kontearen Kantua; Errodrigo Zaratekoaren Kantu Epikoa," *Anuario del Seminario de Filología Vasca "Julio de Urquijo,"* 30-31, 1996, pp. 71-98.

20 "Errodrigok sugarrak bezain agudo egin zuen ihes / Juan Abendaño guduan agertu orduko." Arriolabengoa, Julen, "Erdi Aroko kanta ezezagunak Ibarguen-Cachopin kronikan (1570-1620). Butroeko Andrearen Eresiaren bertsio ezezaguna; Salinasko Kontearen Kantua; Errodrigo Zaratekoaren Kantu Epikoa," *Anuario del Seminario de Filología Vasca "Julio de Urquijo,"* 30-31, 1996, p. 95.

21 *Anuario del Seminario de Filología Vasca "Julio de Urquijo,"* No. 30, Diputación de Guipúzcoa, Donostia, 1996, p. 94.

22 See Michel, Francisque, *Le Pays Basque: sa population, sa langue, ses moeurs, sa littérature et sa musique*, Firmin Didot frères, fils et Cie, 1857. Also, Velasco y Fernández de la Cuesta, Ladislao de, *Los Euskaros en Álava, Guipúzcoa y Vizcaya: sus orígenes, historia, lengua, leyes, costumbres y tradiciones*, Imp. de Oliveres a Cargo de A. Xumetra, Barcelona, 1879, pp. 339-341.

23 Michel, Francisque, *Le Pays Basque: sa population, sa langue, ses moeurs, sa littérature et sa musique*, Firmin Didot frères, fils et Cie, 1857, p. 244.

24 "Apuntamientos de Pedro Sáenz del Puerto Hernani," published by Rafael de Floranes in *De las memorias que tiene la provincia de Guipúzcoa en obras inéditas de Lope García de Sala-*

zar y otros autores publicadas en *1850*. In Isasti, Lope de, *Compendio historial de la provincia de Guipuzcoa, por Lope de Isasti en el año de 1625*, Ignacio Ramon Baroja, Donostia, 1850, appendix, p. 36.

25    https://klasikoak.armiarma.eus/testuak/herri14016.htm

26  *Memorial histórico español: Colección de documentos, opúsculos y antigüedades que publica la Real Academia de la Historia*, Imprenta de José Rodríguez, Madrid, 1834, vol. 7, p. xv.

27  *Memorial histórico español: Colección de documentos, opúsculos y antigüedades que publica la Real Academia de la Historia*, Imprenta de José Rodríguez, Madrid, 1834, vol. 7, p. xv. See also, Mitxelena, Koldo, *Textos arcaicos vascos*, Minotauro, Madrid, 1964, p. 89.

28  Menéndez y Pelayo, Marcelino, *Antología de poetas líricos castellanos: desde la formación del idioma hasta nuestros días*, Librería Hernando, Madrid, 1900, vol. 3, p. 224. See also, Garibay, Esteban de, *Compendio historial de las Chronicas y Universal Historia de todos los Reynos d'España*, Christophoro Plantino, Antwerpen, 1571, lib. 26, p. 300.

29  Carlos, Abelardo de (Ed.), *La Ilustración española y americana*, Gaspar y Roig, Madrid, 1897, vol. 41, p. 102.

30  Fernandez de Larrea, Jon Andoni, "Lucha de bandos y guerra a sangre y fuego," *Anuario del Seminario de Filología Vasca "Julio de Urquijo,"* pp. 697-698.

31  *Memorial histórico español: Colección de documentos, opúsculos y antigüedades que publica la Real Academia de la Historia*, Imprenta de José Rodríguez, Madrid, 1834, vol. 7, p. 46. See also, Mitxelena, Koldo, *Textos arcaicos vascos*, Minotauro, Madrid, 1964, pp. 90-91.

32  Mitxelena, Koldo, *Textos arcaicos vascos*, Minotauro, Madrid, 1964, p. 74.

33  In, https://klasikoak.armiarma.eus/testuak/herri14003.htm

34  Aralar, José, *La victoria de Munguía y la reconciliación de oñazinos y ganboinos*, Ekin, Buenos Aires, 1949.

35 Arriolabengoa, Julen, "Erdi Aroko kanta ezezagunak Ibarguen-Cachopin kronikan (1570-1620). Butroeko Andrearen Eresiaren bertsio ezezaguna; Salinasko Kontearen Kantua; Errodrigo Zaratekoaren Kantu Epikoa," *Anuario del Seminario de Filología Vasca "Julio de Urquijo,"* 30-31, 1996, p. 84.

36 Muxika, Luis M., *Historia de la literatura euskerika*, L. Haranburu, Donostia, 1979, p. 67.

37 Yztueta, Juan Ygnacio de, *Guipuzcoaco Provinciaren Condaira edo Historia*, Ignacio Ramon Baroja, Donostia, 1847, p. 303.

38 https://klasikoak.armiarma.eus/testuak/herri14009.htm

39 Otazu, Alfonso, "El Cantar de Bretaña. Un poema inédito de fines del siglo XV en la lengua vasca," *Anuario del Seminario de Filología Vasca "Julio de Urquijo,"* vol. 7, No.19, 1975, pp. 43-70.

40 Otazu, Alfonso, "El Cantar de Bretaña. Un poema inédito de fines del siglo XV en la lengua vasca," *Anuario del Seminario de Filología Vasca "Julio de Urquijo,"* vol. 7, No.19, 1975, pp. 44-45.

41 Mitxelena, Koldo, *Textos arcaicos vascos*, Minotauro, Madrid, 1964, pp. 75-76.

42 Translation problems set aside, a contemporary interpretation of the song performed by the Euskal Barrok ensemble can be heard at: https://www.youtube.com/watch?v=f4IToZa_9j8. For more background, see the following: Abarzuza, Igor Saenz, "*Jançu janto* y el acto creativo de la traducción panaresca como perversión," *Sonograma: Revista de pensament umsical i difusió cultural*, edizio 044, 29 d'octubre de 2019. This can be read online at: https://sonograma.org/2019/10/jancu-janto-y-el-acto-creativo-de-la-traduccion/. See also, Ansorena, José Luis, "La música en el mar. Itsas Memoria," *Revista de Estudios Marítimos del País Vasco*, No. 6, 2009, pp. 459-478. Also, Barbieri, Francisco A., *Cancionero de Palacio de los siglos XV y XVI transcrito y comentado por Francisco Asenjo Barbieri*, Real

Academia de Bellas Artes de San Fernando, Madrid, 1890. And also, Rey, Pepe, "Jançu janto, una zaloma," *Musiker*, No. 13, 2002, pp. 59-65. Https://kipdf.com/ja-nu-janto-una-zaloma_5ade7ee97f8b9aa41a8b45dc.html

43 Https://vimeo.com/265034787 and https://www.youtube.com/watch?v=bzTLwk1LwY8. Beltxaren Bikotea's version of the song has a helpful explanation before the singing in Basque. The Euskal Barrokensemble's version of this song can be heard at: https://www.youtube.com/watch?v=f4IToZa_9j8

44 Rey, Pepe, "Jançu janto, una zaloma," *Musiker*, No. 13, 2002, pp. 59-65.

45 Mitxelena, Koldo, *Textos arcaicos vascos*, Minotauro, Madrid, 1964, p. 142.

http://www.vc.ehu.es/gordailua/ABESTI%20ELEBIDUNA.htm

46 Because of the suggestion that this poem might be a satirical love song, we've translated it using regular rhyme and meter. In English, it's a six-line poem with four mostly iambic beats per line (standard ballad form in English). Also, since neither an eight-line nor a six-line version replicates the seven lines of the original, the translation is not driven by the idea of the same number of lines.

47 https://klasikoak.armiarma.eus/testuak/testuak15008.htm

48 This may be a reference to the saying, "mucho sabe la raposa (la zorra) y más quien la toma," meaning the fox is crafty but the one who catches the fox is craftier still. We are reminded that we should be careful not to think too highly of our wisdom or knowledge, as there is always someone who knows more than we know.

49 We base the translation of "by his garments of gold" on further reading we've done on Saint Michael who is commonly depicted in full armor—often bronze armor, so golden in color. Also, "bragas" has historically been used not only as underwear but as short trousers and,

in some idiomatic uses, as simply trousers; therefore, we believe the phrase garments of gold gives an accurate picture of the speaker's meaning while avoiding the silliness of swearing by the archangel's underwear.

50   https://klasikoak.armiarma.eus/testuak/herri14013.htm

51   http://aunamendi.eusko-ikaskuntza.eus/eu/canto-del-lelo/ar-80316/

52 Gevaert, Auguste (Ed.), *Chansons du XVe Siècle: Publiées d'après le manuscrit de la Bibliothèque Nationale de Paris par Gaston Paris et accompagnées de la musique transcrite en notation moderne par Auguste Gevaert*, Didot, Paris, 1875, pp. 7-8. See also, Paden, William D., *The Medieval Pastourelle*, Garland Pub., New York, 1987, vol. 2, p. 522.

53 Based on the original language's sense of her speaking quietly and calmly, we'd used the metaphor of the voice like a bell in order to rhyme with the line "…Go, go, time will tell." But we'd then decided "…Go, go, time will tell" wasn't the best choice and translated the line as, "Go, go, time to go," which meant deleting "…gently, voice like a bell." To rhyme with "time to go," we settled on "…gently, yes, could be no." It's nicely ambiguous and allows the young woman's response to grow stronger and clearer as the story proceeds.

54 Menéndez Pelayo, Marcelino, *Obras Completas: Orígenes de la novela*, Universidad de Cantabria, Santander, 2018, vol. 2, p. 932. See also, https://klasikoak.armiarma.eus/testuak/herri14017.htm

55 https://www.deba.eus/eu/udala/udalaren-egitura-eta-sailak/euskara-eta-hezkuntza/debako-kultur-ondarea/alostorrea.pdf

56 Davant, Jean-Louis, *Zuberoako literaturaz. Antologia laburra*, Euskaltzaindia, Bilbo, 2008, p. 5.

57 To hear this contemporary take on the ancient theme, see "Amak ezkondu ninduen": https://www.youtube.com/watch?v=81pgBl0xZzI or https://www.youtube.com/watch?v=RzwEZqQQ76E

58 The link to Antonio Zavala's *Euskal erromantzeak* is: https://www.euskaltzaindia.eus/dok/iker_jagon_tegiak/auspoa/28899.pdf

59 http://www.eusko-ikaskuntza.eus/eu/dokumentu-fondoa/euskal-kantutegia/ab-4998/. See also, Jean de Jaurgain, "Quelques légendes poétiques du Pays de Soule," in *La Tradition du Pays Basque*, Bureaux de la Tradition Nationale, Paris, 1899, pp. 383-385. For a different version of the poem, see, Davant, Jean-Louis, *Ozaze Jaurgainean. Jean de Jaurgainen Züberoa Herriko kondaira poetiko zonbait*, Euskaltzaindia, Bilbo, 2020, pp. 40-41.

60 http://www.eusko-ikaskuntza.eus/eu/dokumentu-fondoa/euskal-kantutegia/ab-3446/

Completed in December 2024
at the Center for Basque Studies,
University of Nevada, Reno.

www.ingramcontent.com/pod-product-compliance
Lightning Source LLC
Chambersburg PA
CBHW030139170426
43199CB00008B/133